# THE COLLECTION
## By Melanie Stephens

*To Makala
With love and best Wishes,
Melanie Stephens x
2021*

Front cover design by Gemma Warne

Back cover photo authors own.

All photographs are royalty free except:

Photos featured in Dinosaur Feet, Joe, Place of Mystery,

The Two Trees, Dedicated to Frances, Forever 36, I Knew a Man, Rainbow, The Rose, Willy & Gert, Woman, Cornwall, Paris, The Greatest Gift, The Opportunity, Weather, Garlic Pizza and Farmhouse Biscuits.

Notre Dame images used with permission from Johnnie and Karen Waugh, Natasha McDonald, and Jackie Eastwood.

All subject to copyright.

For Gavin and our children, Archie, Eliza and Hugo.
M.S.

## PRAISE FOR ISOLATION TALES

 Just completed this compelling book of short fictional stories. Clever uncomplicated text used with dramatic effect engaging the reader from the get-go. These accounts will resonate with many for years to come. An emotional rollercoaster at times but with glimpses of humour to lighten the mood. Undeniably a very poignant book.

I think the mood that's descended on us all is summed up within these pages. It made me think differently about who are, our key workers - the visible and invisible - not only our incredible NHS, but the postie and funeral directors. To appreciate them in ways I never had before. I got a new appreciation for everything.

A brilliant collection of short stories; sensitively written and which really strike the mood of lockdown and the various challenges and sacrifices. I will be hanging onto this copy for many years to come as a reminder of this time.

A book on true life and how people are dealing with the pandemic and coping with a huge change to daily life. Short and quirky stories that in places make you smile. One can imagine being one of the characters. Cannot wait for your next book!

What a pure and real account of this harrowing situation. These fictional journeys are so relatable yet endearing. A truly beautiful writing style. I can't wait to read more!!

★★★★★

I've been enjoying these lovely short stories. Great little read that I highly recommend. Huge extra bonus- Melanie (the author) is donating all money from her book to the N.H.S!!!

★★★★★ I have loved reading this little book. The author shows great insight into the current Covid-19 situation, and the little stories are very entertaining and enlightening. I will definitely keep this book as a 'lockdown' souvenir!

★★★★★ Fantastic book, well-written and enjoyable.

★★★★★ Absolutely superb. I laughed, cried, and felt the power of every story. Loved it! Every word.

★★★★★ Loved this book! Well-rounded stories, poignant and real, but with an approachable easy style.

★★★★★ An emotionally charged book of short stories and poetry. Written, and published during the Covid-19 pandemic and told from the perspective of individual voices and their experiences. From the stay-at-home mum to the firefighters, the nurses, the funeral directors and everyone in between. There is something to make you laugh out loud and then burst into tears. If you're looking for something to showcase the stories of the individual people that have been affected by this pandemic, then this book is definitely for you.

# **CONTENTS**

PAGE

| | |
|---|---|
| 11 | JOE |
| 19 | THE ROSE |
| 21 | LOVE SQUARE |
| 24 | WOMAN |
| 26 | THE GREATEST GIFT |
| 29 | 40 |
| 41 | DANGEROUS FAMILY |
| 49 | EASY WOMAN |
| 51 | NEW BOOTS |
| 53 | DINOSAUR FEET |
| 56 | THE HOUSE THAT MICE BUILT |
| 60 | I KNEW A MAN |
| 62 | A BREAK FROM TRADITION |
| 66 | DINNER |
| 71 | STOLEN MOMENT |
| 73 | CORNWALL |

# CONTENTS

PAGE

| | |
|---|---|
| 78 | THE CHANGE AT 22 |
| 83 | ANXIETY |
| 84 | NOT AFTER MIDNIGHT |
| 89 | TADPOLE |
| 91 | ANA |
| 95 | A JOURNEY OF DEATH AND LIFE |
| 100 | STAR WARS |
| 104 | WILLY AND GERT |
| 110 | ABSENTEE |
| 111 | IN THE HANDS OF THE GODS |
| 117 | BE CAREFUL WHAT YOU SEARCH FOR |
| 122 | PARIS |
| 125 | NOTRE DAME |
| 128 | NOT JUST OLD-SUPER OLD! |
| 137 | TRAIN |
| 142 | FAT GIRL DIARY |

# **CONTENTS**

PAGE

| | |
|---|---|
| 146 | THE SEA |
| 148 | PLACE OF MYSTERY |
| 155 | HOSPITAL |
| 158 | LAST REQUEST |
| 163 | JEANNE |
| 170 | PART 1: THE BABY |
| 172 | PART 2: THE GIRL IN THE CLOUDS |
| 174 | ISOLATION EASE? QUEUE HERE PLEASE! |
| 177 | THE TWO TREES |
| 180 | TWO CATS |
| 182 | GARLIC PIZZA RECIPE |
| 186 | MR. PERFECT & MS.IDEAL |
| 188 | FAME-ILY PHOTOS |
| 196 | FOREVER 36 |
| 200 | THINGS I MIGHT NOT SAY |

# **CONTENTS**

PAGE

| | |
|---|---|
| 202 | THE DANGER OF BEING THE FUNNY ONE |
| 206 | PERFECT WIFE |
| 209 | GEORGE FLOYD |
| 211 | PRIZED SECRETS |
| 219 | RAINBOW |
| 221 | A BAR TALE |
| 228 | EXCLUSIVE |
| 232 | THE OPPORTUNITY |
| 236 | NEW YEAR CONFESSIONS |
| 239 | LOVE |
| 241 | CHAMELEON |
| 243 | THE CHRISTMAS BUS |
| 245 | WEATHER |
| 249 | THINGS I'VE LEARNT AS A MUM-TOP TIPS! |
| 259 | THE GIRL WITH THE GOLDEN HAIR |
| 261 | WOMAN SOLDIER |

# CONTENTS

PAGE

| 263 | SELF SERVICE |
| 268 | TELEPHONE |
| 272 | DEDICATED TO FRANCES |
| 274 | MAIL CRUSH |
| 276 | ATTENTION |
| 279 | DON'T PANIC WHEN DROWNING |
| 283 | BARE |
| 286 | CIRCUS |
| 289 | ALONE |
| 291 | THE MERMAIDS IN THE STARS |
| 295 | DEAR READER |
| 297 | ACKNOWLEDGEMENTS |
| 299 | ABOUT THE AUTHOR |

## **<u>JOE</u>**

It was 11:59 am, one minute later Joe Wilson shut down his computer and started to pack his bag. He did this the same time every day. Joe was the office weirdo, the loner. On the way to the door, he passed two of the graphic designers, Brett and Philip.

'Off again, Joe?' asked Brett. Joe kept his head down and kept walking.

'See ya in an hour, Joe!' Philip called after him.

I walked up to them both. 'Oi guys! Leave him be, he doesn't bother anyone.'

They both stared at me and looked away. Brett turned to Philip, 'our lunchtime and all, eh Phil? Fancy a pint down the Swan?'

'Yeah, mate. Getting a bit fussy around here. Too many women about.'

'Don't be a wanker, Phil,' sniped Suzi from a desk behind them, 'Brendan was only sticking up for his teammate.'

'Yeah, thank God we're not in that team!' laughed Brett.

'Oh my God! I totally wish I was with a graphic designer!' mocked Rachel as she put her hands together beside Suzi, 'they are so cool and dreamy.'

Suzy and Rachel laughed.

'Ha-ha. See you later girls,' Phil called as he led Brett out the door.

'Hey guys! Come on, turn your gear off.' Gerry shouted after them. Brett carried on walking and gave Gerry the finger on the way out.

'I suppose I'll do it then,' Gerry huffed and leaned over and shut down the computers.

'Are you having your lunch now too, Brendan? We might pop into town into the museum café if you wanna join?'

I smiled, happy for the invitation, 'thanks, Suzi. Maybe I will.'

I walked with the girls towards the café. It was a nice one that sold rustic food like soup and baguettes and best of all, lots of homemade cakes. Suzi and Rachel both had a salad and a cake with a coffee where I just had a slice of gateaux and a latte. I'd already eaten a bacon butty mid-morning that my wife sent in. A peace offering. Didn't work. I still ate it though.

'What do you think Joe does every day?' I asked the girls, 'do you guys ever talk to him? Do you know what he likes to do?'

'You sit next to him!' said Suzi.

'Yeah, but you guys have been here longer.'

'I don't know, he's a quiet one. Doesn't he ever talk to you when you are working together?' asked Rachel.

I shook my head, 'only computer stuff.'

Suzi broke off a bit of her cake with her fork, 'have you ever tried talking to him yourself? Small talk even?'

I shook my head again, 'not really.'

'Well, ask to go with him one lunchtime,' Suzi chirped while nudging my elbow. 'See what he says. You never know he might be happy to have some company.'

So that's what I did. The next day I asked Joe where he went.

Joe stared at his screen, 'just around.'

I looked at him, 'can I come with you?'

'Why?' Joe squinted at me, 'are you going to do something?'

I frowned, 'like what?'

Joe didn't answer, he looked at me for a long time.

'Okay,' he said finally after a long pause.

'Today?' I pushed.

Joe shook his head, 'not today. Tomorrow.'

I smiled, 'okay.'

Tomorrow arrived and I watched the clock. I took my morning break early with another bacon butty peace offering from my wife. I was still mad, and tensions were high at home. I started to shut down the computer a couple of minutes early. I was excited and looking forward to it. We left the office.

Brett and Phil were in a meeting in Conference Room B, so no teasing today which I was thankful for. Suzi and Rachel watched us walk out and smiled at me. I pretended not to notice as I didn't want Joe to take anything the wrong way.

Outside, Joe walked down the road the opposite way to the town.

I matched his pace, 'where are we going, Joe?'

'We're walking.'

'Yeah, I know that. Where to?'

Joe kept his gaze down as he walked, 'you wanted to know what I did. This is what I do.'

'Just walking?'

He looked at me, 'nothing is just walking, Brendan.'

We came to a public footpath sign, and he turned beside it. We entered a tunnel of green, trees forming a gateway into nature and all its splendour. A gust of wind blew, and Joe stopped abruptly and took a deep breath as he spread his arms wide and closed his eyes. I watched as the wind undulated his hair.

I tried to make sense of what he was doing but failed. 'Joe, why did you...'

Joe put his hand flat toward me, 'sshh.'

I stopped speaking and waited for him to finish whatever he needed to do. He started moving again after the gust of wind had ended.

'I hear the people I have lost in the wind. I feel them wash over me and speak. When the wind comes, I close my eyes, so they know I am ready to listen.'

'Did you lose anyone close or…'

Joe didn't answer and carried on walking and I followed him slowly. We came to a bench and Joe sat down.

He held his hands together and looked forward, 'Brendan, when you look around you what do you see?'

I glanced around me, there was not much to see, 'I dunno, a few trees, a path, bushes.'

'Do you know what I see?' he asked as he looked at me. I did not answer.

'Life,' Joe continued, 'I see living things. Everything is growing and the colours surround us both. Look at the rainbow around us. The purple of the foxglove, the green of the ivy around the brittle bark of the tree, the beauty of the green in the leaves, the strength of the trunk. We are visiting a part of the world that cannot be replicated anywhere else within Earth or time. Our surroundings are exactly this way but only now. Right this second. We are privileged to experience this and given the chance to appreciate it.'

I looked around us. I noticed a creamy white butterfly as it bounced, playing in the sunshine and I realised what Joe was saying. Right now, this moment isn't taking place anywhere else. This exact moment has never taken place before. I looked at the world with a new lens. I felt such fulfilment, pride, and gratitude for being here. To experience this.

We sat quietly together and took our time to look. Really look. A wind blew and I closed my eyes. The trees rustled and I felt every strand of my hair being massaged, loved, felt. The coolness of the breeze made me feel refreshed and alive. I was silent on the way back and the rest of the afternoon. I felt at peace. There was no use for words. Somehow, I felt I could not explain it to someone where they would understand, even Suzi or Rachel. At least not as well as Joe did to me. So, I quietly got on with my work and looked out the window every now again and saw the colours of the world. I never noticed how intricately the world's palette blended, every view was like a painting. Yet before, all I saw was a few bushes along the road.

I went home that night and kissed my wife. Our disagreement seemed pointless and not worth the words we exchanged. Life was a blessing. I didn't want to waste a single moment I could never get back and I was desperate to appreciate my wife for every second I had her.

We always thought Joe was troubled. That he had upset in his life or was simply weird and complicated being around people. I thought he was feeling hurt after being teased, but Joe didn't answer them back because he rose above it. Joe was never troubled. He had tranquillity.

Two years later, I lost my wife to Cancer. We didn't know she had it, and from the diagnosis to her passing was 6 months. Thanks to the walk with Joe, I had the best 18 months with her I've ever had. If I ignored Joe like everyone else or like I had up to that day I would have taken my wife for granted and bickered over stupid things. Regretting and replaying them constantly in my head, always angry.

I grieved for my Maggie, and I am still grieving. Then I decided to make her proud. So, I set up an IT company with Joe. Peaceful Solutions. We work quietly and happily every day.

Lunchtime we both go for walks. On my walk, I walk alone.

And when the wind blows, I stop. I spread out my arms and show I am ready to listen.

# The Rose

Long Stem

Expanding reach with baby clusters

Jagged leaves

Mother line diverging frail threads

Skeletal under sunlight's beams.

Protective thorns

Concealed present.

Blossoming star

Silky petals

Rich deep red.

A flash of white bleeding into crimson

Textured with beauty

Layered majestic form

More splendour is to come.

Slowly the present unwraps

Reveals a closed centre tightly bound.


Silkiness falls

Tiny dots of blossom under the dying star


Naked green wilting to the floor.

# **LOVE SQUARE**

Alexander hadn't meant for this to happen, things kind of got out of control and now he had to choose. As soon as he turned 36, he felt older, unattractive, bored. He had moved boxes. Whenever there were forms to be filled, you had 18-25, 26-35, 36-49, 50-65, 65+. There was no end after 65. He guessed after that you should just give up and be thankful for every day afterwards.

It started it off with a simple flirtation. At first, Alexander wasn't sure if he had imagined it. But the young guy who he always said 'Hello' to, started stopping a little longer to chat, asking him about his day and what he liked to do. He stood closer to him as they talked and touched his arm a few times. Alexander didn't pull away or flinch when he did. He was tall, muscular and had dark features that made him seem dangerous and more manly.

He found out the guy's name was Paul and he looked forward to seeing him more and more. Whether his hair looked good that week or his dedicated running regime was starting to pay off, the young lad who worked at the shop started flirting with him too. He was a little more forward, holding his hand out to graze Alexander's bottom, which again he wasn't sure if it was a mistake at first. But he didn't pull away. And he enjoyed how it felt, the flutter of wondering, the unknown.

One night, Alexander had gone to the local pub for a community volunteer meeting, Paul was there to join the team after he saw a poster appealing for recruits. He carried a pint of Carlsberg over to the table and sat beside him. Alexander couldn't concentrate on anything being said. He decided to try his luck and moved his leg to Paul's. They were touching. Paul kept his leg there but otherwise didn't respond. Alexander realised he didn't know anything about him. He looked, no ring. Good sign. His heart was thumping in his chest. He had no idea where Paul even lived, obviously local considering how much he had seen him but other than that, he had no idea.

After the meeting ended, they stayed for another drink and took it outside. Then came that moment. The pause, the look at each other for a little longer than fleeting. Alexander could feel his breathing quicken. They both leaned in at the same time, they kissed. It was soft but sensual and left him wanting more. So, they kissed again, and their hands wandered. They smiled at each other and kissed each other again briefly.

'I better go,' Alexander said. Paul replied, 'okay'. From then on, the flirtations were a lot more blatant.

A couple of days later, he saw the young shop assistant outside the shop. They had been friendly for a while, but neither of them had ever made a move. Everything was suggestive. He was also muscular, toned, blonde and tanned.

They said 'hi', and Alexander moved around the trolley of boxes, away from the eyes of passers-by. They instinctively moved in and their lips met, it was exciting, and Alexander could feel his heart beating. It was so unlike him to do any of this. There was nothing before it to signal any of this was going to occur, but it felt exciting and new.

He felt sexy and wanted. He had no idea how young the boy was but figured out he was a great deal younger. He walked home happy, but also a little nervous if anyone saw.

A week later, on social media, Alexander saw his old flame and messaged him to say hi. A simple greeting turned to flirtation and it got even heavier. The messages were becoming more and more risqué as they described in detail what they could do to each other. Soon, he was asking to meet, which Alexander was unsure about.

Time went on, and Alexander sunk deeper. He kept on having flirtations with Paul and the shop boy, but he felt things were getting out of hand. And now here he was wondering how to stop everything he had started. It was fun, exciting and he loved how each of the men saw him. But he knew none of this was healthy. He turned his wedding ring on his finger. It would all make sense if he weren't in love. But he loved being married, the flame was still strong, he was just…he didn't know.

At night Alexander's husband, Wyatt came home from work and greeted Alexander and their daughter Audrey with a kiss and a smile. Alexander played the loving husband role well, it felt strange at first after the forbidden kisses and intense flirtations, but he felt confident he wouldn't be found out. The indiscretions felt reckless, guilty, he made more loving gestures towards Wyatt hoping that would blind him to what was going on.

Alexander knew things couldn't go on the way they were. He wanted to be good. He just had to remember how.

# Woman

Whatever happened to women and children first?
Why must we rely on Mrs Pankhurst?
You expect us to serve you, be silent and clean,
After all the horrors and injustice we have seen?

No! Give us our freedom, you must do what is right,
We deserve equality! Or we will continue to fight.
Torture and ridicule us, we will just pursue,

We believe in ourselves; we believe in the truth.
We will revolt! Destroy windows! Burn buildings down!
Anything needed to accomplish our plan.

I wear this sash 'Votes for Women' with pride.
I trust in our cause with duty in mind.
The police are brutal, abuse is rife,
They do not see I am a Mother. A Daughter. A Wife.
I march with my banner, proud of every step I take.
It marks a sisterhood, a movement I choose to partake.
Women will have a say, we will win their respect.
There will come a time when we can write 'X'.

Emily, you did not die in vain, the vote we will get.
Generations will remember our sacrifices as a Suffragette.

Women of the future, Flee! Go to the ballots with great haste!
A Vote, our gift to you, is too precious to waste.

The best protection any woman can have is courage.
ELIZABETH CADY STAUNTON.

*When my son was little, he loved the Pip & Posy series by Axel Schaffer. The books are unique by they deal with worries and problems of toddlers, which seem simple to us but mean so much to them. Each story was incredibly charming and ended with a 'hooray!' which my little boy loved.*

*There are very few, (in fact, this is the only series I can think of) where the stories are aimed at children two to four years. It is that in-between stage of being too old for baby books but too young for the 3-5 target market.*

*I wrote a letter explaining how refreshing it was to have stories aimed specifically at this age group. They replied, enclosing a soft toy of Pip, and asked if I would be willing to write a post for the Publisher Nosy Crow's website. I was honoured to be asked and called them straightaway. At time of print, it is still on the website. But to save you searching, here is that post. I hope you like it.*

The greatest gift you can give a child is the joy of reading. And the best time to start is at the beginning. As soon as my children were born, they had a cloth book and a bath book.

You'd be amazed how early babies can turn a page.

A favourite with all three of my children was *Peepo* by Janet and Allan Ahlberg. The rhyming repetitive words create a natural melody, speaking to a baby's love of music. The child also recognises one of the most instinctive games parents play with their babies. Peek-a-boo.

Every book you read with them benefits your child. Books with large flaps encourage independence, books with textures encourage the baby to explore the world around them, and one of the best series for 2-4-year olds is *Pip and Posy* by Axel Scheffler.

Each story seems simple but is completely relatable to little toddlers and is presented in such a fun and friendly way. Falling off a scooter, losing something new or forgetting your favourite toy. They also cover the early stages of friendship, learning to say sorry and how to help others.

Books are more available than ever before. It has never been easier to share that special moment with your child. Turn off the world and share the experience. Laugh at the funny bits, cheer with the hoorays at the end, and get sad when things go wrong. Have fun with stories and your child will want to hear them again and again. Take books with you wherever you go, and you will give them a love that will last a lifetime.

# 40

The dreaded day had arrived, there was no stopping it no matter what I did. Thanks to an over-excited Aunt and the biggest picture the site allows with a big 40 on it, my morning routine of checking out Facebook and laughing at memes of misbehaving cats has turned into a bloodbath of people I haven't seen in 20 years wishing me many happy returns now I am old. I already know it will only get worse as the day goes on especially as I realise when you join, you enter your date of birth. Even people who don't see the photo from my over-enthusiastic Aunt will be reminded by Facebook of my landmark number.

    I drag myself out of bed and look in the mirror. I swear six lines have appeared on my face overnight. And so, it begins, a lifetime of wrinkles. It's official- the life of carefree youth is over. And I am positively pissed off that I have now entered the land of no return. Any lbs I put on will take twice as long to get off. No more worry-free cakes and flavoured cappuccinos in Costa, everything has magically doubled in calories. I am doomed to elastic waists and comfortable shoes.

    I go downstairs, thankful I am in a marriage where we share everything. We gossip about people the other person does not know, and I have exhausted myself informing him about my hatred for my upcoming birthday. Surely my husband will be thoughtful and considerate over my feelings. Wouldn't he?

    I open the lounge door and am greeted by a gold inflated 4 and 0 that is roughly the size of half my body. What the fuck are those?

I stare at them, willing for them to undo and whizz around the room making farting noises. No such luck. My two daughters rush in.

'Mummy! Happy birthday we got you balloons! '

'I see. I could hardly miss them!'

My traitor of a husband comes up and kisses me, 'the girls thought it would be fun.'

I raise my eyebrow, 'and they knew my age, how?'

He grins, 'I may have let it slip.'

I give him a look and he disappears into the kitchen returning with a glass of bubbly. At least he knows me a little bit then.

'Here, darling,' he says passing me a glass. 'The girls also made you breakfast.'

Piss ants. There goes my fry up. Yep, walk into the kitchen and soggy cornflakes and a slice of toast with a clump of butter and more holes than a cheese grater is waiting for me.

Surely, they don't expect me to eat it.

'Lovely,' I lie through gritted teeth. Already my mind is working into overdrive planning to throw the lot in the bin and get started on my real breakfast. Unfortunately for me, the criminals to the world of culinary masterpieces sit down.

'We want to stay with you mummy and watch you enjoy every mouthful.'

Of course, you do. For fucks sake!

I bite a bit of rubbery cold toast and try to give a convincing smile. Not my best work. Thankfully, a quick grimace doesn't go unnoticed, and my husband finally gets how much I am not finding this cute. Even the girls' big brown eyes and long eyelashes are not convincing me to enjoy it.

My husband gives an unnaturally high-pitched laugh. 'Oh! We haven't given Mummy her presents,' he says quickly, leaving the room and rushing upstairs.

The girls follow and I seize my chance. I rush over and scrape the lot into the bin. I vow to hit McDonald's after dropping the girls off at school.

The presents are smellies, Disney Princess perfume and a bloody Dyson. Pathetic. I was hoping for a new laptop for work. The girls and my husband ignored hints, went to Boots and took advantage of our Prime membership on Amazon. I wonder if the idiot knows Amazon also do laptops. I know I mustn't be ungrateful, at least they remembered. I probably need to be more obvious in my hinting. You know, hey remember all that talk about laptops and how much I would love one? And how they make great presents for landmark birthdays? I meant me! BUY ME A LAPTOP!

'Harry's wife has one and says it's amazing. Makes hoovering so much easier. I thought you would like your life to be less hassle. Cause you know that's what you're always saying.'

I hate Harry's wife. She sounds like a moron.

'They cost a fortune you know.'

I stare at him and wonder how much 'a fortune' is. I will go on Google later, and price comparison the Dyson to a laptop.

'Well, time to get ready for school, girls,' attentive hubby announces.

Please don't go, at least get them ready so I don't have to. He grabs his bag... God, it's so annoying he just leaves.

'I hope all my girls have fun today,' he says kissing me on the cheek. 'Have a great day babe. My cougar.' He leaves, laughing at his own joke. He is three months younger than me; he makes the same joke every year. And only the first time was it remotely funny.

His duty is now apparently over and no doubt he will expect me to put out tonight as a 'birthday treat'. I take a deep breath. 'Right girls, you heard Daddy, let's get you ready.'

I follow the girls upstairs to their bedrooms to get them ready for school. Even though it is my birthday, it is still something out of a hostage scene with me playing the role of negotiator and failing miserably. I look at my watch and curse, as we are now 10 minutes late from the bell. I will have to drive them. I bribe them into the car with Haribo and take the short ride to school. We pull up, and I park diagonally across two spaces. I can't be bothered to straighten up. I quickly look around to see if there are any witnesses to my aversion to lines and order the girls to rush into school reception.

'Out partying last night to celebrate the big 4-0, eh? Naughty! Naughty! And on a school night!' Bollocks! It's Ted, the school leech. He has a natural talent to make anything sound dirty. Dad to a lovely quiet girl in my eldest daughter's class. Always acting like a single man, trying to chat everyone up. Strangely, his wife thinks he's hilarious. Every joke is sleazy, and his view is getting closer and closer to my chest as he powers them off one after another. Maybe he's ageing badly and his eyesight's going, and he needs to lean in to get a good look. Whatever the reason, Ted's a creep.

I try to think of some witty comeback but can't be arsed, and just laugh a little politely. 'Morning Ted.' Little does Ted know, last night consisted of me making coffee, half drinking it and falling asleep on the sofa whilst my husband watched television. What a wild night indeed!

I get in my car, and head for McDonald's. I pull up in a space in the car park, reach to grab my purse from my bag which I then realise I left at home. Bollocks!

Back I go, deliberating whether an Egg McMuffin is worth all this effort. Especially when I am having lunch out with some mum friends. I decide it isn't and eat a cupcake from the treat box instead. I'm old, I deserve it. I was given a bloody vacuum cleaner. I decide to eat two cupcakes and, just to be healthy, also half a tub of blueberries and a litre of coffee.

Time to head to lunch. I use Sat Nav as I have not been here before. When I arrive, I see why I have not been there. It is one of those hippy new age places with couscous salads and tiffins. It's the kind of place I hate. No tables, just long benches like in the PE class at school. Impossible to get in and out of unless you are familiar with yoga position 134: Café gecko with nofallonass backwards. I am the first one at the table, I look at the menu and see they serve fucking cereal. What the hell? Who does that?

I look beside the till and thank the Lord when I see they have a cake selection. And they do sandwiches. Mmmm bacon!

The women I'm meeting all come in together like a rabble of those annoying birds at the zoo.

'Emilia!' they all say at once so it's impossible to know who to answer. I decide to answer collectively.

'Hi, girls.' I cheer and stand up, knocking my leg on the wood. It hurts.

They give me a group hug. Like, all at once. I look around to make sure nobody saw. After all, we're not American.

'You're all here at once,' I say trying to figure out how they did it.

'Well, we all met after school drop off and went for coffee,' explains Jackie, the leader and therefore is always looking for gratitude and attention, 'none of us wanted to be sat here by ourselves. It looks so lonely and sad.'

Ah, the big fear of the young. Most need to hold another hand just to go to the bathroom. I'm guessing it hasn't occurred to her that she just called me lonely and sad. Or maybe it did and she's a bigger bitch than I thought.

'We would have asked you along too, Emilia, but I guess we missed you,' Jackie continues.

They all look at me waiting for my response, they already know I was late or at the very least, heavily suspect it.

I plaster on a fake smile, 'that's okay, we are all here now.'

They all sit down, somehow with ease and quite smoothly, apart from Jill who struggles to get her legs under the bench. I thank God for Jill. She's in just as much trouble as I am.

'Emelia, you may wonder why we asked you to lunch today,' Jackie said coyly.

I look at her wondering if it was something other than my birthday. Weren't we here because it was my birthday? When she approached me about it first and I was too tired to think about an excuse not to, didn't she mention my birthday?

'Well,' Jackie looks at the other mums and continues, 'a little bird let it slip it was a special day for you, and…'

So, it is about my birthday, what is this?

She says Jill's name, I think discreetly. Or meant to be.

Jill passes over a gift bag and a massive card.

'Happy Birthday!' Jackie announces, Jill and another mum, Maisie, try to join in and say it too but shy away when Jackie gives them a hard look.

Fake surprise, fake surprise, fake surprise…I plaster on a big-over-reaction-of-shock face. 'Oh my gosh thank you!' I say, taking the bag and giant card.

'Don't open them yet. We must order first,' Jackie commands me.

A waitress, obviously waiting for her cue, walks over, 'hello Ladies, what can I get you?'

'Just a courgette salad for me,' said Jackie.

I look confused. Courgette salad? Why pay someone to make you that and then eat it?

'I'm vegan,' Jackie explains, 'And watching my weight.'

I know what she's waiting for but I'm not feeling charitable. She stares at me waiting to see if I'll cave. Thankfully, the waitress butts in,

'The courgette salad isn't vegan. It has parmesan, mozzarella and quail eggs.'

Jackie stares at the waitress, 'just leave all that out.' She snaps.

'Okay, but that would only leave you with mixed salad leaves, tomatoes and courgette. Is that okay? Cause I will still have to charge you the full price.'

'Fine,' Jackie gives the waitress a death stare and holds out her menu.

'You can just put that back on the table.' Touché waitress. Touché.

'Can I have the mushroom omelette please with salad?' asks Maisie.

'Just Weetabix for me,' said another mum, Terri.

I always hated you, Terri. You freak.

'Would you like yoghurt and fruit on that?' the waitress asks.

Oh, that sounds interesting.

'Yes, please. Greek honey, blueberries, raspberries and strawberries.'

'Anything on top?'

' Manuka honey?' Terri replies.

What the hell? The massively expensive one, is Terri out of her mind? They would never agree to that.

'No problem,' confirms the waitress.

I've always loved you Terri, you absolute genius.

'I'll have the same,' I tell her and smile at Terri who smiles back.

'I'll have a chicken burger with the works,' orders Jill. We all look at her. 'I'm on 5:2. Today is a 2.'

We all bob our heads in acceptance of Jill's explanation.

The waitress makes a note, 'and drinks?'

'Orange juice for me, please. And water for the table,' said Terri.

'Shall we order bubbles?' said Jackie, 'a little cheeky Prosecco?'

'Aren't you all driving?' I ask them, gutted I can't join in.

'We all came in Terri's car,' replies Jill.

'I have a spare seat,' adds Terri, 'if you want a drink, I can drop you back later when it's worn off.'

Terri, you are a magician and now easily my favourite, 'My husband has a car, he can bring me, and we can get it later. That's amazing, thank you.'

'Well, it is your birthday,' Terri smiles. I love her.

'Well, that solves it. One bottle of Prosecco and four glasses please,' Jackie said excitedly.

I pull the waitress's sleeve, 'can I have a large glass of red wine?'

She smiles and says, 'sure.'

'In fact,' I say holding on, 'leave the bottle.' Might as well, it's not often I get a free pass.

The waitress makes a note, 'did you still want four glasses for Prosecco?'

'Oh yes,' I tell her. This lunch could end up being half-decent after all.


'Emelia! Why don't you open your card now?' Jackie instructs me after the waitress had gone.

I give a polite smile and open a massive card with a big 40 on it. There is a picture of a girl riding a motorbike over a mound of grass. With the slogan Feeling over the hill? Be grateful you're not under it.

Jackie starts laughing, 'I know it's a little naughty, but it is amusing don't you think.?'

Umm. No. But it is annoying they are all either below or in the early 30s. To them, I'm about to collect my pension and according to the card, I should be thankful I'm not dead.

Only Jill and Jackie have signed it. Which means there's probably more of this to come. I look around for the waitress. That wine's taking a while, isn't it?

'Thanks, Jackie and Jill,' I say through gritted teeth. I turn the card over to see a 99p sticker from Card Factory, the greeting card shop in town. Even more depressingly, Jill works there and gets a staff discount.

I look in the gift bag and see a candle with 40 on it, a big glass with a giant 40 on it- seriously, who buys these glasses? What is the point of them? And oh no. My heart sinks.

I kid you not, a giant pink round badge with a massive 40 on it. The badge is bigger than my face. I just realise I am wearing a silk red shirt. Fuck. They wouldn't, would they?

Please, please, please, please… don't make me wear this hideous badge!

'Emelia! Put it on! Let's see it!' Jackie teases. There is no doubt now, she is a bitch.

'I'll put it on later,' I say sweetly. Maybe when hell freezes over, or they invent a time when bright pink doesn't clash with red.

'Don't be silly! This is your birthday lunch. Don't you want to show everyone how old you are? Get them all to wish you a happy birthday? You are only 40 once.' Yep, a Class. A. Bitch.

'I would Jackie, and I am grateful, but I don't want to put any pinholes in my shirt, you see its silk…'

'You don't want to disappoint me or Jill, do you?' Jackie canters.

'You can use it as a stand too, so you don't have to pin it to your blouse,' Jill interrupts.

Relief. 'And that's what I love about it the most Jill. Thank you.' We exchange smiles. And now I am filled with gratitude. Bless you, Jill.

Red wine comes to celebrate my narrow escape and Terri looks a bit worried when the rest of the bottle is left beside me. I'm also handed a glass of Prosecco.

'Don't worry, I don't throw up when I'm pissed. Your car is safe,' I inform her.

She chuckles and says 'Phew!' and then reaches down and passes me a card. Maisie reaches into her bag and does the same.

'Thanks, guys, you shouldn't have.'

'They had to as they didn't come in with our card,' said Jackie.

'We didn't know about it, that's why!' protests Maisie.

'Well, that's what happens when you don't 'WhatsApp'. I mean, really girls, who doesn't WhatsApp!?!' teases Jackie.

'If only we had a way to see each other every day? Like, you know, school times?' I point out. Maisie and Terri giggle behind their hands avoiding the dreaded Jackie's gaze. I open Terri's card. A basic happy birthday with flowers on it. It is my favourite so far.

I open Maisie's next. Glitter glue and confetti burst over my jeans along with two test tubes of gold glitter.

'Halle wanted to make your card,' Maisie announces like a proud parent. The card is quite cute apart from all the shit that fell off it. Albeit a bit random. Its main feature is a cat in a field with a panda and a unicorn. And for some reason a guy suspiciously like Simon Cowell is hovering in the background.

'She loves cats, unicorns, pandas and the X-Factor. Sorry, she did spell your name wrong. But you know kids!' laughs Maisie.

I look inside after clogging my hands with glitter and confetti. I tilt and shake it towards the floor and get death stares from the staff in the café. The card was made out to 'Ebola'. Who knew, it was also the birthday of a deadly virus? Another reason to be cheerful and to celebrate.

Jackie obviously was feeling weak after not having any attention for five minutes and decides to talk loudly and get as many glares as she can from all the other diners. 'Raise your glasses girls. To Emelia. Happy birthday, we hope it is at least one to remember.' Then sneakily adds, 'We know you haven't got that many left.'

We clink glasses. I think it is debatable I will remember this one, Jackie.

Especially as with every spoonful of Weetabix, I am happily washing it down with a juggernaut helping of my old friend Chianti. Cheers!

# DANGEROUS FAMILY

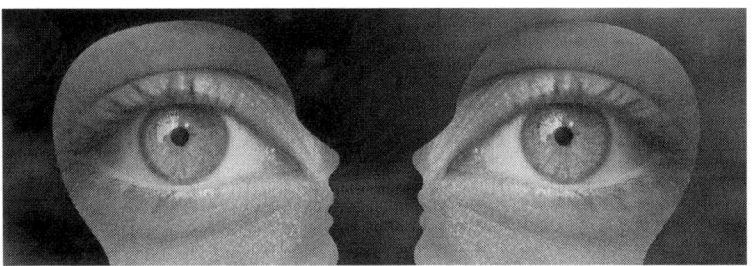

**Calvin**

I wake up. Today is the day. I must act quickly before she stops sleeping. I pack my bag and check my list one last time.

Comic-check.

Sock-check.

Toothbrush-check.

Keyring from the railway in the shape of a train-check.

Spare trousers-check.

I have everything I need. It's time to go. I walk to the door. It is locked. But I know where the key is. It is in her bag. Last night she forgot to take it upstairs, I saw it in the kitchen. I walk to the kitchen and find the bag. It is on the table. She was foolish to forget it.

I rifle through, moving my hand amongst papers, tablets, secret plans, her purse, and makeup. I find the key. I take it and move towards the front door. I pick up my backpack. I hear a noise. It could be the wild dog she keeps up there to stop me from leaving. I must be faster.

I take the key and unlock the door. It opens. I am in the back garden. There is a wind chime hanging from the tree. It is my wind chime. I want to take it with me, but it is dangerous as it makes noise. I pace from one foot to the other until I decide to slip it into my bag. It chimes as I do, and a light comes on in her bedroom window. I must leave now, or I will never escape.

I go to the side of the house and climb over the gate. I race along our path across the lawn. I zoom down the road. I feel like my legs will fall off. My breath is fast.

'Calvin! Come back!' I hear her shout behind me.

Soon she will release the wild dog. I hear barking. It's happening, I must move faster. I look around for anyone who might be able to help me.

There is no one. I rush to town. A fire-truck is parked outside the church next to Costa Coffee. They must help! I go to the truck and bang my fists on the door.

'HELP ME! OPEN UP!' I shout. They open the door.

A big man, who is wearing a costume, I think his name is Bruce or Grayson opens the door and steps down.

His voice is deep. 'Hey, are you okay? What's the matter?'

I realise I have not blinked and blink my eyes lots of times. 'Please help me! A woman is holding me prisoner. She is keeping me locked up. I've only just managed to escape! Please help me! Call the police! Keep me safe please!'

'Okay, don't worry, I'll help you. Where do you live?'

'I don't know where she keeps me. She keeps the location hidden!'

The Bruce Grayson man puts a hand on my shoulder, 'it will be okay. Where is she now?'

I look behind me and see her, 'she's chasing me!' I tell him. 'She's coming now! You have to help me!'

'Okay, mate. Don't worry, I won't let anyone hurt you. You're safe now.' Bruce Grayson opens the door and tells his friend to come down. There are men in a row behind them too. Bruce Grayson picks up his radio and reports a possible kidnapping. I climb into the fire truck and wait.

'CALVIN!'

'It's her! Oh my God! It's her!' I shout, pointing.

'It's okay mate. Stay here.'

Bruce Grayson walks to her and they talk. He is blocking her view of the truck. She is shouting but I cannot hear what she says. The men in the row behind are talking but I cannot hear what they are saying either. They are all huddled together as they chat. I see Bruce Grayson and her are walking here together.

She's tricked him. I need to go. The fireman is blocking my exit but the side with the steering wheel is clear. I move along the seat fast and open the door. I rush out quickly and move as fast as I can. I bump into a fireman carrying something on fire and he burns me as I crash into him.

I push him as hard as I can and keep running fast. Firemen are chasing me along with the woman who wants to kill me. How can they fall for her lies? I knew she was good but good enough to fool Bruce Grayson?

I dart through the alleyway and make abrupt turns for several miles. I think I have lost them. I hear a siren in the background. They are all chasing me and brought in reinforcements. I must be smart.

'Calvin!' She has found me.

How? Of course, the cameras. I forgot about the cameras. How stupid of me. I throw my backpack on the floor. I must leave it behind. She had more resources than I realised.

I press on forwards, across a field where I am an open target. If she has followed my trail, she could shoot me right here. My heart is racing with every step. I zig-zag in the hope to make it harder for her to aim.

'Calvin!'

I suspect she expected it to distract me long enough so she could find her target, but I do not give her that chance. I have made it! Calls still come in from behind me and now I come near the quay, I might be able to fool her that I have drowned in the water.

No, she knows I can swim after she tried to drown me two years ago. I get to the little stone beach, there is a fire that has burnt out, so it is a mould of black. Bottles are around it. Pirates and smugglers, I expect. I take a glass bottle and throw it against the wall. It smashes as I hoped. I lie in wait. My moment is coming, I must be brave, or I shall never be free.

**Margaret**

I hear birds tweeting outside, I wake after a terrible nights' sleep. I have just been packed with worry as usual since I brought Calvin home. I don't know how I thought I could do this. I will have to tell Michael tomorrow that he will have to go back with them.

I try and get a couple more minutes sleep which of course never works. My dog Fred is sleeping on the bed with me, the great lug. I should say no, but I am so glad to have some company and a bit of affection, so I give in.

What was that noise? It sounded like a clatter of bells. I turn my light on to get a better look and walk to the window. Clumping sounds are beside me. Someone's outside. I look in the lounge, Calvin's backpack is gone. Shit! He's trying to run.

I quickly unbolt the front door and look out across the lawn. I see a glimpse of his backpack down the road.

'Calvin!' I scream. 'Come back!' I knew I needed better security. I rush back inside and take out some leggings and a top from the laundry basket. I search for my bag and find it in the kitchen. That's how he got out. Damn it! I should have been more careful. I head out the door and hurtle down the road.

I get into town and down the main street. I can see a fire-truck outside the Red Cross shop and Costa Coffee. Calvin is talking to a fireman waving his arms.

Bloody hell, the last thing I need is someone else being involved. I scream at him, 'CALVIN!'

Calvin gets in the truck. Shit. And here comes Mr Hero.

'Morning Ma'am. How are we doing today?'

What an idiotic question, 'peachy.'

'The young man seems quite upset. He seems to think you are holding him against his will.'

'I am his mother.'

'Can you prove that?'

It always astounds me how perfect strangers demand explanations about your parenting. I force a smile, grab my bag, and find my purse, handing him my drivers' license. 'Here you go,' I hold it out for the fireman. 'He's not well, I need to get him home.'

The judgemental fireman stares at my licence not looking up, 'in what way is he not well?'

'In a head way. He's mentally ill,' I snap.

'He seemed fine with me.'

And the judgement just keeps coming. Of course, he seemed fine, always does in the first ten bloody minutes. 'Well, he's not fine. Look I need to give him his medication. You can stay with me, just get the authorities to call Michael at Paradise House. He'll explain.'

'Okay ma'am, come with me.'

We walk to the truck but then I lock eyes with Calvin, I know he's going to bolt.

Shit. Don't run, don't run, don't run…

He's opened the door. Fuck. One of the firemen getting a round of coffees for the team comes out of Costa holding two trays filled with cardboard cups.

Calvin crashes right into him and coffee spills everywhere. He pauses, flinches then speeds off. I follow as Mr Hero helps his teammate, 'hey!' They call after me. I keep chasing.

Calvin passes the shops and down an alley, he moves around all over the place, his usual route, and I find his backpack and put it over my shoulder.

He sprints over the big patch of grass before the Marina where he climbed on a boat and slipped off two years ago. Of course, it was my fault. He goes on the pebbly beach along beside the wall and then huddles down by a black patch where someone must have had a bonfire the night before.

I stop walking. He's not moving, neither am I.

'Calvin?' I try. He doesn't move.

'Calvin, you have to come back.' No response.

'You're not well love.' Still nothing. I have no idea if I am getting through.

'You have to come home.'

Motionless.

'Michael can come back, and you go back to Paradise house? If you want to leave, you can. It's no problem.' There's no reaction to anything I say.

'Darling. Come on. I'm your mum I would never do anything to hurt you. You're my son. You need to take your medication. But you can't run away like this, people think horrible things. '

I look at my son and wonder how long it has been since his brain was well. When did he last know how much I loved him? Did he know I miss him so much I begged the hospital to let him live with me? How much I had to fight for that to happen? How much I want us to be together? Has there ever been a time when he felt love? When was the last time he called me Mum?

I walk slowly toward him and place my hand gently on his shoulder. He flinches dramatically like I am made of ice.

'Calvin, I love you.'

As soon as I utter the words, he turns, a flash of his arm and a sharp pain enters my stomach. I instinctively press my hands upon it and they immediately soak in red. I look at Calvin in horror and I see my scared little boy, his eyes empty. My eyes fill with tears.

His arm moves again. And a new sharp pain comes, it's excruciating. My stomach feels like an oven. My clothes are wet, I can feel them sticking to my body.

'It's not your fault,' I manage but I feel so tired. 'I love you.' I try to reach out but the last thing I see is my son until he fades away to nothing I recognise.

I hear sirens. I sleep.

# EASY WOMAN

My skirt is high, my legs are long.

My tops are low, I burst into song!

Looking for attention. **Hey! Look at me!**

The men and my friends smile, they like what they see.

They call me a *slut* because of one kiss,

But there was kindness behind it, a reason they miss.

The man was crying, he needed a friend.

I gave him a boost-

a one-off event.

But other eyes saw different and started to talk

They started to sneer and make fun of my walk.

They do not see my life bound by gold,

When I took my husband to have and to hold.

Twenty years together, the only man I want.

My heart is his, not risked for a jaunt.

I told him of the kiss, it was on the cheek.

My compassion was strong, my will was not weak.

I dress how I wish; I dress only for me.

I ask for nothing but indifference, *please let me be*.

49

You want me to think about you, as your husband stares

*'There is that heartlet, all couples beware!'*


Well, guess what, your ignorance and petty gossip will cost you dear.

Because I am a loyal friend, one who will stand beside you, no matter my fear.

I am dependable, generous, and thoughtful to all.


If only you hadn't made up your mind so quickly and let your mask fall.

## NEW BOOTS

I have some new boots
They are white up to my knee,
I want to show the world
The sexy new me!
The boots clip when I walk
I smile as people glance.
Excitement fills my feet
And I do a happy dance.

A lady says, '*Oh, nice boots!*'
I Cheshire grin and say, '**I KNOW**!'
And quickly add, 'Thank you!'
Before I clip and go.
I buy a dress for my new boots
I do believe they've earnt it!
For making me feel fabulous
Everywhere I stand and sit.

I love my new boots so much
I don't want to take them off.

But then it gets to bedtime,

And I am once again a dwarf!

*HOORAY FOR FASHION AND FANCY SHOES!*

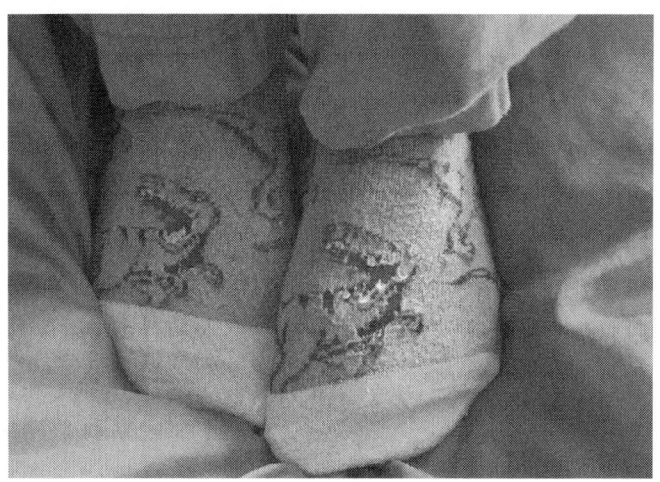

## DINOSAUR FEET

It was morning and after eating his cornflakes in his favourite bowl- the one with the big Dinosaur at the bottom; Dougie peered at the dinosaur's feet. They were huge bumpy things that to Dougie just looked ugly. And scary.

He looked at his feet. They did not look like the dinosaur's feet. They were small and smooth. He had little toes. But as Mum said, Dougie was still growing. Maybe after growing his feet would be like Dinosaur feet. He looked at the Dinosaur's hands. They were small. He looked at his hands, they were small too.

Noises came from upstairs. Daddy was up.

He slid off his chair and put his bowl on top of his favourite bucket. It was safe in a place that he could remember when he came back down. He might need the bowl for further inspection.

He ran upstairs and could hear Daddy humming inside the bathroom. Dougie opened the door and walked inside.

'Morning Dougie,' greeted Daddy in between hums.

'Hi,' Dougie replied and ran to Daddy's bare feet. He crouched down to get a closer look and leant in towards the toes. His little mouth gasped. Daddy's feet were like the Dinosaur!

But worse, they had hairy bits too! Daddy's feet were less green but long claws were on each toe.

Daddy stepped back. 'What're you doing there, mate?'

Dougie didn't answer and ran downstairs to look at his bowl again. He remembered it was on top of

his favourite bucket, but when he got there it had gone! He scratched his head and tried to think hard. He walked back in the kitchen and saw it beside the sink. Dougie grabbed it and looked at the picture of the dinosaur again. Daddy definitely had dinosaur feet. He must hide it better this time so he can keep looking in case Daddy had other Dinosaur developments.  He looked in the garden and saw Mum hanging out the washing. He had to seize his chance. The bowl was placed in the fridge behind a bag of carrots. The bowl was orange and so were the carrots. Dougie felt like an expert hiding person who was also very clever.

He sat down and thought. He did not want dinosaur feet. Daddy came downstairs in clothes for work. Dougie looked at Daddy's feet. They were hidden in black socks and no one could see the monster toes inside. Socks are most definitely needed to stop the dinosaur developments.

He ran upstairs again and opened his sock drawer. There were lots to choose from, including ones with dinosaurs on. Dougie separated the dinosaur ones and decided to put them in Daddy's sock drawer. It was too late for Daddy, he already had dinosaur feet. He could have those. Dougie found a nice pair with stripes and a tractor on. That's better.

Dougie kept his socks on all day.  Now and then he would take his bowl out of the fridge from behind the carrots and check his feet were still small and smooth. The socks were working, his feet stayed the same. After looking at his bowl, it was put back behind the carrots. Mum asked him where his bowl was when she washed up at teatime. Dougie decided to run away pretending to be a lorry. It was naughty to lie.

It came to bath time. He took off his clothes as Mum ran his bath. Dougie sat down on his feet so Mum couldn't see his tractor socks were still on. Mum lifted him into the bath and the phone rang.

'Oh, it's probably Grandma. Stay still!'

Mum ran downstairs, Dougie had to hide his socks. He found flannels and covered his socked feet. Mum was on her way. She was holding the phone to her ear when she came back. Dougie grabbed lots of toys scattering them around his feet. Mum talked on the phone as she quickly washed him. After he was rinsed off, Mum said to get out.

Arm outstretched, he pointed his little finger directly behind her, 'look! Over there! It's a big rabbit!'

As his mum looked, Dougie quickly got out and covered his wet socks with the bathmat. They felt a bit squelchy now and a bit stuck. Dougie didn't want tractor feet. Although the wheels would be good for hurrying about, he would not be able to wear his fire truck wellies anymore, and he liked those a lot.

Wrapped snugly in a towel he ran to his bedroom, quickly took off his wet socks and hid them under his bed. He replaced them with bright pink socks from mummy's sock draw. He would have to think hard what to do about it all tomorrow. Dougie felt quite tired now, it was hard work keeping his feet small!

This story I wrote for my Aunty Zoe and Uncle Chris, they were going through a particularly hard time and I wanted to give them something that might help. I wanted to show that even when our world feels like it is crumbling around us if we have love and each other, then we have everything.

## **THE HOUSE THAT MICE BUILT**

Once there was a little mouse called Zoe. She was small and cute, and everyone admired her. She liked to make things and give them as presents to people she knew. One day, Zoe met and fell in love with a big handsome mouse called Chris. He was also kind and thoughtful, and everyone marvelled at how in love they were.

Once, they took a walk across a field and they saw this lovely house. It was old but exceptionally beautiful. They knew at once this house is where they would make their home. They built themselves a charming little house inside this striking building. It made them both smile at how proud they were of the life they had built together. Soon their lives became even richer, when they had four babies, a small amount by mice standards. And in time, the mouse babies had babies of their own.

They loved being together, having tea with little teacups. Their favourite thing was being outside where the children could run. They would go in the field where they first saw their home and shared memories of how their life began. A favourite tradition was to have these delicious farmhouse biscuits that they made as a family every Sunday.

The mice family's life was idyllic but there was a problem. The house wasn't safe. Sickness took over and made it dangerous to live in. The house needed to be restored, but first everything needed to be destroyed.

The beautiful house that caught their eye was almost falling apart, but the little home the mice built was strong. It was made with so much love that helped it thrive. Love is the most powerful thing known to the world; it has the power to create, but also to devastate any threat. Nothing can ever diminish it.

They knew for a while they had to stop going outside and could not do the things they normally could. Sometimes they had to brave the world in their little garden, especially when a new wave of demolition commenced. They sensed the big house coming down around them and they worried the world they knew was falling apart. In a way it was, but when the desolation was complete, amongst the rubble the charming little house remained. They could not rebuild a new house with this other little house in the way.

No matter how much they tried to pull down this little house, nothing could injure it or get through. The mice were frightened and scared, but still, their little home survived and protected them. The walls held strong and stayed together. They were indestructible. Nothing could destroy their home. It remained full of love.

In the end, they had no choice but to build the new house around them. And it was magnificent.

The mice family had made it through. For a while, the world they knew had gone astray, and all that was left in their entire universe was this tiny house that two little mice built. It was small but it was perfect. Zoe and Chris felt like they could do anything, beat anything. They enjoyed creating that little home and the little house they built would stand there till the end of time. The family welcomed more mouse babies into their home and then even more. The house made room for everyone.

Generation after generation. The world they built lived on forever. They were always happy, and they always cherished and protected the most powerful thing they had. Love.

*This is the recipe for Farmhouse biscuits; the ones the mice family made every Sunday.*

*Try them, they are delicious!*

## FARMHOUSE BISCUITS

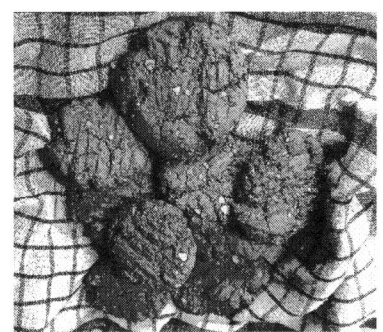

**Ingredients**

*100g/4oz spreadable butter*

*75g/3oz caster sugar*

*1 tbsp cocoa*

*150g/5oz self-raising flour*

*75g/3oz porridge oats*

*½ tsp vanilla essence*

Set the oven to 150 degrees C, 300 degrees F, Gas mark 2

Beat the margarine and sugar together. Sieve the flour and cocoa into the mixture. Mix it all with the oats and vanilla essence. If it is too crumbly, knead the mixture by hand.

Roll small amounts of the dough into balls between the palms of your hands. Arrange them on baking trays and flatten each one with a fork. Do not make them too thin.

It doesn't matter if these biscuits are uneven in size.

Bake in the oven for 35 minutes, lift and cool on a wire tray.

# I Knew a Man

I knew a man who gazed at me with love. His deep blue eyes, the shade of perfect seawater being the first sight I see.

I knew a man who filled me with joy and laughter every time we met. His strong arms keeping me safe.

I knew a man who would speak of love and admiration for his beloved, keeping her memory alive around me. Helping me to know her in his view, showing me snapshots of the moments, they shared.

I knew a man who made porridge every day. Have it bubbling every morning on the stove, as I do now. A gentle nod to the man I loved.

I knew a man who believed a garden was a place of nurture and pride. Creating a paradise of plants and vegetables, feeding a family from his own bare hands. The simplistic pleasure of a garden bench.

I knew a man who rejoiced when he learned of me becoming a wife, jumping up to shake my suitor's hand. His approval I craved above all others.

I knew a man who, when he held my first babe in his arms, tears pricked his eyes. And when he learnt they would share the same name and he was the inspiration to guide my son through life, the tears travelled down his cheeks.

I knew a man who never saw darkness within his fellow man. He only spoke of good; things to be thankful for and how our arms and minds should always be open.

I knew a man who took a piece of my heart.

I remember how leaving that room was the hardest thing I ever had to do, knowing it would be the last time we would ever be together. I held your hand and kissed you for the last time.

I knew a man who shaped me. He taught me love, friendship, laughter, and simple pleasures.

I knew that man.

He lives on within me.

This story was inspired by a newspaper clipping about a man in China (newspapers are a great source of story ideas). It was for the end evaluation of a writing course tutored by fellow author, Elaine Johns. As well as a brilliant teacher and talented writer, Elaine had a successful singing career with her husband and twin brother (for UK fans he plays Charlie in the long-running medical drama, Casualty). Hope you all enjoy it.

## **A BREAK FROM TRADITION**

Kazuko looked out the window. Even by day, the lights of Tokyo overwhelmed him in a sea of spectral colour. He glanced down; flashes of light invaded his gaze. He closed the curtain. Kazuko looked across at his soon-to-be bride. A work of art he thought. Beautiful in her way, she sat obediently on the bed waiting for instruction on what would happen next. A piece of red cloth laced with gold was draped beside her.

'They will be camped out at the Registry Office too now Mai. We must prepare for the whole world to see us.'

Mai sat quietly and said nothing in return.

'Say something,' Kazuko ordered.

'Something.'

Kazuko smiled. It always made him laugh when she did that. He thought of their journey together and the carefree two months dating before he decided to risk everything so they could marry. Filled with controversy, all his family apart from his mother had disowned him in shame. His friends and employees understood, they too were hounded and pressured by their parents to get married. Mai might have not been their first choice, but he searched for a more respectable spouse. He just couldn't find one! He did love,

Mai. She would never leave him, she belonged to him, and could be trusted to respect him, she couldn't cheat, and therefore never hurt him. Soon he would teach her how to be a wife. How to cook and clean. She could be everything he desired. What other wives could do that? He made Mai into the woman she is today; she was his creation.

Kazuko looked at the clock, 'see the time. Not long now.'

'Seven minutes and 33 seconds.'

'Yes. Thank you, Mai.' he rubbed his hands into his trousers as he sat down beside her. 'This is a big step for me. All the photographers out there waiting for us.'

'Would you like me to call a taxicab?'

'Yes, Mai. Thank you.'

Mai made the call, 'one is on its way; it will be here in 7 minutes. The driver said five, but it will be 7. '

Kazuko smiled. The bride is always late. He lifted the red cloth from the bed and placed it softly over her pale face and long auburn hair. His mother would either appreciate or be disgusted with him for keeping with her Chinese traditions. He stood and looked out the window.

'The taxi is here,' he said walking over to her. 'Here, let me lift you.'

Kazuko wrapped his arms under Mai and lifted his future bride, so her head fell onto his chest. Her painted mouth peeked out from under the red veil. He carried her out of the room and down the short burst of stairs to the front door.

'He's coming!' he heard someone shout.

Flashes of light blinded him as he stepped outside. He held Mai close to him and the taxi driver came round and opened the door. He kept his head down as he got Mai settled on the back seat and then himself. Questions flew toward them from every direction, but he could not decipher any of them. In under 8 minutes, they had reached their destination. A crowd quickly formed around the car as they arrived. Kazuko got out and pulled Mai across the seat towards him.

They rushed inside, barging their way through the sea of bodies and cameras surrounding them. Kazuko's mother was waiting along with his work colleagues. Among them Lei, his best friend. Lei saw the red veil and smirked.

As predicted Kazuko's mother was horrified. She ran up to him as he carried his future bride. 'Please, Kazuko. Think before you do this! It will bring a big shame to our family. You are making a mockery of us all.'

'I am doing this, Mother,' he replied, 'you always wanted me to get married. You should be happy it's to such a nice pretty girl.'

'She is not a girl! That thing is a doll. Marry someone living!' she retorted.

'She is a mechanical being…' Kazuko began.

'A robot!'

'Okay, a robot. But soon to be my wife. I created her. With my own hands. I programmed her…' Lei, his friend coughed. Kazuko took the hint, 'okay, with a little help from Lei. But she is mine! You should be happy! You drove me to this. It wasn't enough I was top of my class. It wasn't enough I work in one of the most prestigious labs in Tokyo. No! Just nagging! Get married! Find a wife! Well, I couldn't find one. So, I had to build one. '

'Kazuko! If…' his mother began before a man appeared and called down the corridor. 'Kazuko Wang and Mai please.'

Kazuko strolled past his mother who quickly followed along with Lei and his work colleagues from the lab.

They said their vows exactly as Kazuko had prearranged and when the register and certificates were signed, Kazuko told Lei to invite the press in. A rumble of noise of world-wide vocabulary entered the room, as it filled with hungry eyes and flashes of light. Kazuko clutched his new wife proudly and addressed a sea of Dictaphones as they were plunged towards his face.

He told them how he would soon programme her to walk and do chores but for now, he would carry her. He explained about the pressures put upon him to find a wife, and how his fellow stressed lab partners rejoiced when he told them of his solution. After fifteen minutes of questions, the journalists were ordered out so Kazuko and Mai could get their things together and leave. His mother had already left without a word, and when Kazuko asked his new wife how she felt about today, Mai gave her one-word answer.

'Perfect,' she said.

Just as he had programmed her to.

# **DINNER**

Gareth had never cooked a chicken before, today he was attempting three. After a loss of knowing what to do and a faint recollection seeing lemon and garlic flavoured chicken in the supermarket, he had stuffed two smashed bulbs of garlic and half a lemon in each. He saw an opening and guessed that was the one he needed. There was a moment of schoolboy curiosity when he wondered whether a chicken would stay on his hand if he kept it inside and lifted it. Gareth pushed his fingers and palm into the cave of lemon and garlic, tried one and then both. He saw his neighbour George in the garden next door who waved hello. Gareth waved back with both hands, a smile turned into a quizzical look from neighbour George.

Gareth quickly realised he had chicken hands and ducked with a girlish scream. He placed both chickens on the chopping board and removed his hands from inside. Gareth slathered all three birds in butter using his palms and fingers. There was an overwhelming urge to run his hands over his face and hair. Which he did. He was going to have a shower later anyway, and the family was coming over. He was preparing for war, so he might as well look the part. He heated up the cooker, put all three chickens inside and slammed the oven door.

The potatoes were next. He tried peeling them, but as tiny little strips came off, he thought this was going to take forever. There was still butter on his hands making them greasy, so the peeler kept slipping through his fist like a fish. Several times it flew over onto the cooker. He washed his hands and got a knife whilst grunting,

'Man's knife,' he said to thin air.

Gareth then had the brainwave of making them rustic, 'Skins on,' he told the air with more grunting. He chopped them in half and put them in a saucepan to parboil them. Then he started on the veg. 'More rustic,' he informed the air and just chopped clumps of any vegetables he didn't have to peel.

Broccoli. Gareth's favourite. He tore the florets off the stalk, 'Man. Warrior. Make food,' he grunted, again to the air. He enjoyed himself so much, he did another one; he ripped it apart, the same way as the first.

He poured all the veg into a long deep roasting pan he borrowed off his mum and took out the sprouts from the fridge. The sprouts were easy, in a bag all loose. He just sprinkled these on top and then remembered he had a bag of peas in the freezer. He took it out, and as it was in a big clump, he started whacking it against the worktop. The strategy of hit and hope worked, and the peas separated. He ripped the bag open and poured them over the tray. Some were in clumps with ice but as it was just water, he thought this was fine and got his spice rack.

The spice rack was a housewarming present when he got his place four years ago and was still in cellophane. He took the plastic wrapping off and looked at the labels. He wasn't too sure which ones to use so he decided a bit of everything was the safest option. There were lots of different colours in the rack so he was sure it would taste of something. By the time the herbs and spices were finished, there was a thick layer of topping on the veg. Gareth stared at the pan hoping for inspiration. He thought it might be a bit dry, so he scraped his fingers over his face and delved into the concoction of veg mixing everything together with butter. For the second time since he started that morning, Gareth washed his hands. He drizzled everything with oil and covered it with foil as he thought that's what Gordon Ramsay would do. Pleased with how professional it looked, he set the veg aside.

The potatoes were part boiled now, and he drained the water in a colander. He discovered the thin strips of potato peelings had also been boiled but Gareth decided this could only add extra flavour and add to the rustic vibe of his menu. He shimmied the boiled skins and potatoes into a roasting pan and then wondered what to put on top. He decided on more butter and started splodging clumps into the pan, sprinkled some salt and pepper on top and added more garlic and all the green coloured herbs he had in the rack.

Afterwards, he thought it was looking fairly good and Gareth was pleased with himself. He shoved the potatoes in the oven, made himself a cup of tea and settled down to watch something on Netflix. Unfortunately, Gareth's choice of viewing was a thriller and he had forgotten to set the timer. After forty minutes, he realised he had no idea how much longer he had to wait before putting the veg in the oven. He decided to start cooking the vegetables now.

He opened the oven door. There was no room, even when he tried using the grill tray, he had used up most of the space with the three chickens. So, Gareth decided the best idea would be to balance the tray of vegetables in between two of them. Very slowly he placed it on top of the meat and lightly moved his hands away, so he did not disturb the light force around the food pyramid structure. The tray slipped down almost immediately and collapsed spreading raw vegetables all over the kitchen floor.

'Shit!'

Gareth quickly got on his knees and started scooping up all the vegetables he could find putting them back on the tray. Gareth could see a cluster of vegetables including a lot of the frozen peas had landed on top of a little heap of his dirty washing. It was crumpled, waiting to go in the washing machine in front of it.

Carefully, so the vegetables didn't touch his boxer shorts any more than needed, he prized the carrots, peas, broccoli and sprouts away and put them back in the pan. Some sprouts had super flown as far as under his dusty radiator. Gareth looked at the soiled green spheres and wondered what to do. His mum never taught him to waste food, so he blew on them and tried throwing each one in the pan. He missed, and some ended up on top of his underwear, so he picked them up and reunited them with the others.

After one last look on his hands and knees, he got up.

'Ow! FUCK!' The bang on his head made him realise the oven door was still open and he rubbed his head erratically, forgetting he still had butter in his hair from pretending to be a warrior.

He looked at the arrangement inside the oven door and decided to try piling two chickens on top of each other. He picked up one chicken.

'Fucking hell!' After discovering chickens get hot in ovens, he decided oven gloves might be useful. Looking around, Gareth could not see his oven gloves or remember if he had any. So, instead, he grabbed two tea-towels from the kitchen cupboards.

The heat was still burning his hands, so he worked fast. He piled one chicken on top of another slightly leaning it to the side of the oven. He shoved the veg in and quickly closed the door. There was a clank, but he decided to ignore it.

Gareth realised he had not yet made gravy. He took out the gravy granules from the cupboard and boiled the kettle. He didn't like instructions and decided to wing it. He filled about a quarter of the jug with gravy granules and added boiling water. It became a kind of thick paste. He added more water, but it was still gunky. Gareth filled the jug up to the top and mixed it with a spoon, but it wasn't looking quite right.

Next to the sink, he spied a big empty vodka bottle he and a friend finished the other night, and decided to try that as the top was still with it. Using the jug, he put the gravy mixture into the bottle, topped it up with hot water from the tap and shook it wildly.

'Not bad,' he said to his friend 'thin air', but pointlessly wondered if he should have washed the bottle first. Gareth put the gravy with an alcoholic edge into the fridge and watched the end of his Netflix programme. It was a thrilling series with every episode ending on a cliff-hanger and so he watched the next one too.

Ding Dong!

Without thinking, Gareth opened the door. His mum and dad were greeted with their son in stained boxers, buttered hair, shiny-faced and his knees covered in a kind of mush of red, brown, orange and green stuff. Not to mention the very questionable smells coming from the kitchen. His dad started laughing at the sight of his firstborn, and his mother startled dropped the bottle of wine that she was carrying for the meal. Standing in silence, Gareth finally invited them into the massacre that awaited them and his sisters.

This story generated a big response when I published it on my Facebook page. It resonated with so many and such kind feedback was sent to me. This happened to me in real life, and sometimes I think it's good to share even your most personal moments through the written word. So many of us feel it's not good to talk about such things, but what it does is help others not to feel so alone. The realisation someone else feels the same way is such a comforting thought.

## **STOLEN MOMENT**

I pick up my plate of carrot cake and cappuccino and head toward the comfortable sofas, sit down and sink, feeling the seat mould itself around me. I turn to my left and see Grampie pretending to fall, making himself laugh. Mum is chuckling beside me full of giggles at my Grandfather's little routine. My brother, who is a quiet laugher, sits next me; his shoulders are shaking. We smile at each other; my brother only shows this side of him to a blessed few. He laughs so easy in our company, his deep blue eyes twinkling.

Grampie settles down to drink his cup of tea, we look around the Cornish Café. Flags strung across the eaves provide bunting for the proud locals and a little flavour for the tourists. We all coo in appreciation as we tuck into our cakes. Grampie, a traditionalist, enjoys his slice of Victoria Sponge; Mum, who is always on a diet, chose lemon cake. She believes the fruit description alone makes it healthier than any other options. She glares at me for having carrot cake as vegetables are better for you than fruit. My brother has a chocolate muffin as it's easy to eat.

Cream teas are our usual treat but for some reason today its cake and…

'Excuse me, is anyone sitting here?' The stranger wakes me from my daydream.

I look around at the empty spaces around me and the chair she wants to steal as well as my memory.

I shake my head.

She takes it away thanking me.

Grampie, Mum and my brother have gone. I am alone. The only one left. A tear rolls down my cheek before I can catch it. The feeling of acute loneliness and my solitary presence overwhelms me.

Some teenagers sit on the sofa beside me, having fun, being friends. They are young. I envy their innocence, wishing I could bring mine back. I quickly drink my coffee and leave, deserting my favourite cake as nausea fills my stomach.

I re-join my family at the park, my body feeling heavy, my children and husband are waiting for me. They call my name. They are happy, smiling, living life. Just as they are meant to.

I smile through the pain; my husband sees through my charade and rubs my back. We sit in silence as we watch the children play.

# Cornwall

As stunning a place Cornwall is, there is also a code in Cornwall that no one speaks of. It is the Emmett code, which is Cornish slang for tourist. If you live in Cornwall, you belong to one of these camps:

1. Born in Cornwall, along with your mother and father.
2. Live in Cornwall but born somewhere else
3. Cornwall is not your first home and you are the spawn of Satan
4. If you were born in Cornwall, moved upcountry (which describes anywhere the other side of the Tamar) but you saw the light and came home back to your roots.

When meeting a Cornish person and strike up a conversation, if you fall into camp 1, you are immediately accepted if you can tell where your family are from and especially if you have a mutual person in common. You will instantly end up with a new friend and have an hour-long conversation about how brilliant Cornwall is and how lucky we are to live here. If you let slip you come from a string of Cornish generations, then you are 'True Cornish'. The number of generations you need differs throughout the County. I have always believed it to be five, but I have come across others who have other ideas.

If you fall into camp 2, then although you get described as local, to the Cornish person, you are never described as Cornish. This is an unspoken rule that everyone seems to know apart from anyone who falls into Camp 2. There is an opportunity to rise to furriner status, but you need to have lived in Cornwall for over twenty years to achieve that social standing. Even if you were a baby when you moved, the Cornish don't care.

If you fall into Camp 3, no one likes you.

Villagers and Cornish town folk hate empty buildings. It is depressing seeing little businesses being forced to close, as they cannot afford to keep them running all year round. Having half the town/village in darkness just because Cornwall isn't good enough when the sun's not shining is believed to be insulting. If you are in Camp 3, you are not the most popular kid in school.

Camp 4 is complicated. Try telling your story to a local and there's a big element of I told you so in the response, 'I could have told ya not to bother. Can't get better than Cornwall.'

Now, you might wonder, what's all this about? Why do these guys think Cornwall's so special? The reason is simple. It is. Cornwall is a paradise which is why the Cornish are so fiercely protective of it. Surrounded by beaches and coastal walks, history, gorgeous countryside, and farmland, it is a lovely place to live with sensational views.

Sure, the wages are low and house prices are high. It also rains a lot, but even when it does, it is draped in landscapes that go on for miles. Each little village has its own character and ways. Every inch of the county is deep in folklore and legend. The magic of the Cornish Piskies, the miner's tales, the farms going back centuries. And that is not even mentioning the big pull. The part of Cornwall like no other. The Sea. Crashing waves, sun-kissed surfers, fresh fish, expeditions to see dolphins and sea lions, even the city of Atlantis is believed to be lost under the Cornish ocean beside Land's End.

The National Trust protects the Country's beauty spots and for such a small part of the world, many sites are based in Cornwall as there are so many breath-taking places to visit.

Although the Emmett code exists, the locals know they could not survive without the tourists coming in. Sure, the A30 is avoided like the plague come any kind of school holiday; they drive inappropriate cars for the country roads (and never reverse into a passing place and we can't talk about the Cream tea horrors when people do it the wrong way- there is a fierce rivalry between Devon and Cornwall over scones. When you have a cream tea, the Cornish place a dollop of jam on the scone and clotted cream on top. The Devon people put jam on top with the cream underneath. It is painful to watch!) but every villager is aware tourism is a necessity. So, tourists will always get true hospitality. Locals will chat with anyone like a cousin they see now and again. They will give you directions (if you can understand them, most locals go the more scenic route), tell you how to make the most of your stay through places to visit whilst you're here and wish you a safe journey home. They might even encourage you to buy a shell necklace on the way out.

It may seem that the Cornish see themselves as a separate entity to the rest of the country. And that is because, again, put simply, they do. Cornwall was separate from the rest of the country for centuries. Independent. 500 years ago, the country of Britain was widely described as being inhabited by the Englishmen, Scots, Welshmen, and the Cornish people. Even in the mid-16th century, the Cornish still had their individual customs, practices, pastimes, and style of clothing. They even had their own language described as the Cornish tongue; classes are still taught to speak it today. But as with Latin, many have just ended up talking English, which is a lot more practical especially for this day and age. But as with the feeling of being a separate entity, the county is trying to hold on to the dialect and keep a degree of it in force. They decorate each destination sign throughout Kernow with the Cornish translation.

One of the best things about living in Cornwall is food and drink. Pasties are a thing of beauty, and nowhere does them justice apart from Cornwall. Saffron cake and buns, Cornish Clotted cream, Cornish Yarg, Cornish Mead, cider, and ale taste like no other. And if you go to a fishing village where a café or restaurant serve it, you can even have fish and chips with Cornish potatoes and fish caught that morning. Food and drink are massive! Everywhere you look there are festivals, vineyards, breweries, and bakers. And that's not including family recipes like Raw Tatty fry, fish stew, Stargazey pie or heavy cake.

The myth and legend involved in Cornish history show a side of mystical magic. From Knights, giants, dragons, mermaids or smugglers, there are always plenty of tales to tell around a campfire on a sandy beach. Because its unique surroundings and heritage it explains why so many creative people have been inspired here. Daphne De Maurier, the Newlyn school, John Le Carr☐, the Minack theatre, so many elements of culture. There are so many great festivals that happen throughout the year including St Piran's Day, The Padstow Food Festival, Obby 'Oss, Flora Day in Helston and Trevithick Day in Camborne. Nothing quite brings in the crowds like the Royal Cornwall Show, the Boardmasters Festival or the Mousehole lights at Christmas.

For me, the reason I love Cornwall and wouldn't live anywhere else is simplicity. Nothing means more to me than sitting on the beach or walking anywhere beside the sea. Feeling the fresh breeze flow gently through my hair, the taste of saltiness upon my fingers and lips. I couldn't live anywhere else because of the untouched beauty. The picture-postcard views and the contentment I feel with my arms around the people I love, capturing the moment in memory so I can store it in my heart.

So, if you do come to Cornwall, always remember jam first but more importantly, don't rush. There is nothing that cannot wait whilst you take in and appreciate the beauty of your surroundings. Live like the locals and take your time. You'll get round to it dreckly.

# **THE CHANGE AT 22**

The flowers looked expensive in the shop but now as Tina looked closer, some appeared limp and lifeless. She had chosen a big bouquet, knowing more is better, especially where her mother was concerned. She also bought her a book which her mother would probably never read, and a CD of love songs she would probably never listen to. What a charade! Every year they go through the same thing, but it was easy. Thankfully, this year Tina had a plan.

The number 22 bus pulled into the Edgeware Road stop and she got on. It was packed as usual, but thankfully she spotted a spare seat next to a lady holding a brown paper bag on her lap.

'Do you mind?' Tina asked as she approached the lady.

The lady shifted a little along the seat. 'No, of course. Please, sit down.'

Tina sat down first and let her bag including the cd and book hang from her arm. The flowers now seemed to take up every inch of space in front of her, even protruding on the lady's part and the cellophane brushed against the paper of her bag. Tina flushed and gave her an apologetic smile.

The lady smiled back. 'Beautiful flowers.'

'Thank you. They are for my mum.'

'Special occasion?'

'It's her birthday.'

'Oh, lovely. You must be close, it's a gorgeous bouquet.'

Tina shuffled in her seat. 'Not really. We have a sort of love-hate relationship. I go more as a matter of duty. I asked my friend to call with an emergency. That way, I only have to spend an hour with her. That will mostly be her sorting out the flowers and small talk. I can handle that.'

The lady looked down, fished around in the pocket of her coat, took out a tissue and wiped her nose. 'Is she really that bad?'

The bus pulled up to the next stop. An old lady came on with one of those trolley bags on wheels. Tina worried for a moment she would have to move but she found a seat near the front. She turned back to the lady sat beside her.

'My mum left us all. Moved out. Just like that. Her and my dad were married for thirty years. She just up and left. I know she's an adult but how selfish. There was four of us at home. I know we are all grown up, but it still hurt. Tina stared at the lady and waited for a reaction. The lady just nodded.

'She hardly ever cooked,' Tina continued, speaking a little more briskly. 'I remember weeks of the same thing day after day. I would come in after my swimming lesson to leftovers! She couldn't even be bothered to cook for me. And always in my business. Asking where I'm going, who I'm seeing and why. It's so bloody frustrating. And since she left Dad, she is so competitive with me. Copying everything I do. '

The lady smiled.

Tina looked out of the window and breathed out heavily, 'do you know what she called me? Valentina! Valentina! We live in Devon, not frickin' Italy! She saw this programme on TV and decided just like that. She named me after some random woman! I suppose she liked the name. Valentina Treshca or something. My dad wanted to call me Sophie. At least that's normal. I make sure every person calls me Tina. When I have kids, I am going to call them less embarrassing names like Jane or Paige.'

The lady reached into her paper bag and took out a satsuma, 'would you like one?' she asked Tina as the bus pulled into another stop.

'No, thank you.'

A heavily pregnant woman got on to the bus and a young man with a green backpack gave up his seat and stood in the aisle holding on to the pole.

The lady put the satsuma back in her bag, 'the fruit and veg shop in town sells the best satsumas. No pips and easy to peel.' she said smiling.

Tina smiled back. The lady turned in her seat so she could see Tina better.

'Listen, dear, I don't know your mum or you. But it does occur to me that your mum is rather brave.'

Tina wrinkled her nose. 'Brave? How did you get brave out of all that?'

'Was your mum working when she left?'

Tina frowned. 'No.'

The woman leaned slightly closer. 'So, your mum left all the security of a marriage and a home to start a new life after over thirty years? She left her children, not knowing how to pay her bills. She must have been unhappy for a long time if she waited until you were all grown.'

Tina looked down at the floor of the bus.

'I expect she was scared,' the lady continued, 'didn't know what to do with herself. When people are at a loss, they look to who they admire, who they want to be, to try and set goals. Your mum saw you. You are perfection to her. What she dreams to be. How wonderful that she sees you in that way.' The lady's tone was warm and soft. 'Tell me, when you had leftovers, were you at the start of a new term with swimming lessons?'

Tina looked at the lady and thought as their eyes set on each other, neither of them blinked. 'Umm...yes.' Tina admitted.

The lady leaned in toward her ever so slightly and looked at her straight on. 'When there is a new term, you have to pay for that batch of lessons upfront. I suspect your mum had to batch cook that week so she could afford them.'

Tina flicked her head toward the window of the bus, her eyes glistened.

'Don't feel bad. I was just like you. I was angry with my mother. She just gave me away. My adoptive mum always let me know I was adopted, and as far as she knew my real mother was married in a good district and was middle class. I could never understand it. And I was so angry all the time. Why did she let me go? Why didn't she want me?' The lady looked down at her hands, her arms folded around herself. 'When I was 18, I did some digging. My mum had it right, my real mother was middle class. But I found out she was also in an abusive relationship. Her husband was a monster. He knew she was pregnant with me, but he was away with work when I was born. My mother gave me away to a loving home. When he found out what she did, he beat her so bad she never recovered and passed away. He killed himself soon after.'

Tina gasped, 'I am so sorry! Please, don't think about it.'

The lady smiled and wiped away a tear before it reached her cheek. 'She liked clementines and satsumas like me. I visit her grave, sit down, and eat them. I know that might sound daft, but it's my way of touching base with her. We catch up and I tell her all about Julie, my adopted mum.'

The lady leant over and pressed the stop button. Tina got out of her seat to let the lady through. The lady stood up, holding the metal pole for support.

The bus pulled into the side of the road beside the bus stop.

'Valentina Tereshkova was the first woman in space. She was Russian not Italian. If I were you, I'd be proud to have a name of such ambition and that carries so much pride. Say happy birthday to your mum, and I hope you enjoy your hour with her. '

'Thank you,' said Tina.

The lady shuffled down to the front of the bus and got off.

Tina moved into the lady's seat and rested her bag on the chair. She reached in and grabbed her phone. She went on to messages and began to text. She smiled.

DO NOT CALL AT 3 PM. I WANT TO SPEND SOME TIME WITH MUM. WE HAVE LOTS TO TALK ABOUT.SPEAK SOON, VALENTINA X

## Anxiety

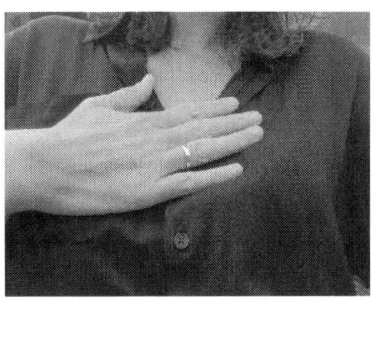

Pain in chest

Bad thoughts

Heart racing

Sweating

Dizziness

Finding it hard to breathe

Can't concentrate

Panic

Can't stay still

Tightening in chest

I'm so scared

Eyes look for help

Blockage in throat

Hyperventilating

This is the end

Squeezing arms

Trying to breathe

Take deep breaths

Breathe... This has happened before... Breathe...

You can handle this

Breathe... Just breathe... Breathe... Breathe... Breathe...

Still.

This story was my entry for the 2020 Fowey Competition. The theme we were all given was 'Not After Midnight'. I am part of a writing group which I love, the other members are brilliant and it's nice how supportive we are of each other. As a group, we all entered the competition and it's amazing how three words could inspire so many different interpretations and ideas. If you are a writer or aspiring to be, I fully recommend local writing groups as you feel so motivated after each meet and you then have writer friends which is wonderful. The story didn't place, but it was interesting theme to write.

## **NOT AFTER MIDNIGHT**

'Sorry. It's the only thing they had. I've had them on these trains before though, it tastes okay.'

Charlotte took the vegan brownie from Kai.

'Where's yours?'

Kai sat down beside her and pulled down his little fold-out table placing the brown paper bag on top.

He passed her a cardboard cup, 'that was the last one. And I'm afraid it's black coffee, no soya milk either.'

'Doesn't matter. Did you want to share?' She asked, holding out the brownie.

'Sure.'

Charlotte opened the brownie and broke it in half giving the slightly bigger half to Kai.

'Our last meal together. Shame it's not better, I should have thought it through. Made it more romantic.' Kai gave her an apologetic smile.

'It's fine. Reminds me of college, I never had enough milk, so I always drank black coffee.'

Charlotte and Kai nibbled the brownie, it was dry but full of cocoa. Charlotte's mind ran back over the last ten months and the first time she saw Kai. His naturally tanned skin, deep brown eyes and a smile that made her instantly drawn to him. His broad shoulders and chest snug under his pale blue shirt.

Kai noticed her amongst the other tech freelancers straightaway, her long red hair hung loosely around her shoulders.

Charlotte was chosen to show Kai around as they both normally lived a long way from Cornwall. She had already stayed two months in the historic village of Charlestown, famous for filming and coastal walks around the harbour. The two of them were staying in the Pier House, it had great views and a restaurant and pub downstairs. The rest of the freelancers were in the Rashleigh Arms.

Kai was covering maternity leave for ten months until the Manager returned to the Cornwall branch. Eros IT Solutions or EIS had so many customers travelling up from Cornwall to London, they thought it made sense to set up a Cornish branch.

They met for dinner that first night and they both flirted. Kai turned up dressed in a t-shirt and jeans and waited as he savoured a pint of the local brewery ale. Charlotte came down in a short denim skirt and jumper.

They kept the meal casual, fish and chips for Charlotte and stir fry vegetables with salad for Kai.

The next night, the freelancers gathered for a pub quiz at the Rashleigh Arms and invited Kai along.

Before they realised, Charlotte and Kai had spent four consecutive nights together. They would talk about the differences between home and here. In London, you kept to the people you knew, everywhere you ventured in Cornwall, people spoke to each other. Every stranger was a friend. It felt odd, to begin with, but after a day or two, they found themselves doing it too. Popping into the local café and having a chat about the weather.

Charlotte loved Adam, her fiancé but they had been together a long time. It was no longer exciting, the sex was predictable, it always lasted longer because he didn't seem as excited by her anymore like he used to be.

Kai was different. They had this amazing spark. It drew them together and for a while, they could not get closer without touching. She watched his mouth, stared into his eyes, those amazing blue eyes.

'There are lots I want to say but I shouldn't,' he told her one night.

She desperately wanted Kai to say them. To reassure her she wasn't imagining the attraction. Charlotte could make sure, but there was so much risk. It would mean endangering the life she had built. Her relationship with Adam was the focus of that.

They began to flirt outrageously but kept it suggestive. Charlotte became vegan around him, to make him like her more. The personal space between them grew smaller and smaller. Charlotte could feel her heart racing as they were close enough to kiss. It felt dangerous. Wrong but also incredibly sexy.

After the dinners and pub drinks, Kai would walk her to her door. These moments had become longer and longer.

'Do you want to come in?' Charlotte would ask.

'I better not.'

'It's okay on the doorstep, but I have a family. A wife. You have a fiancé.'

Charlotte had never been so tempted by another man. He had everything she had looked for when she was single. Perfect. Adam was none of these things, which ironically was the reason she fell in love with him.

Kai held magnetism. She reasoned with herself she could see how far to push the boundaries. Not do anything, just indulge a little.

Charlotte normally loved hearing from Adam. She counted down the hours and minutes until they would speak again, but she began to find the calls a nuisance.

She started to dress a little sexier, hoping Kai would notice. He did.

Kai started finding ways to touch her. Charlotte liked tempting him. She enjoyed it, it made her feel powerful and desirable. There were so many times she wanted to kiss him. She would watch Kai talk, the way his tongue moved.

They resisted for a long time. But then, one night, things changed.

'Do you want to come in?' Charlotte asked. She always did out of politeness.

'Just for a bit,' Kai said.

Surprised, Charlotte opened the door. As soon as he stepped across the doorway, they couldn't control themselves any longer. Their hands explored. Their lips met with urgency and intense craving. But even then, he stopped.

'I can't do this. I'm so sorry.' He left.

Charlotte understood. Kai had more to lose, more hearts to break should they ever be discovered.

Kai did not see Charlotte the next day. She heard him on the phone to Zara his wife. Presumably reminding himself of his other life. But their attraction could not be contained and the following night, Kai did not stop.

Every night after, the affair continued. Planned evenings turned into fleeting moments when reality visited.

And now here they were, maternity leave and the freelance contract completed; they were sat together on a train back to London. It arrived in Paddington at midnight which would mean the end. Not after Midnight. They had both agreed.

Two hours and fifteen minutes remained of the affair. They had finished the brownie and black coffee and sat quietly.

'I know we agreed to never say it,' Kai said breaking the silence. 'But I do love you Charlotte, you will always be with me. I will always think of you.'

Charlotte smiled. 'Me too.'

She wanted to hold his hand but decided not to. They were coming to an end. All the affection between them had been private. And that's how it would remain. A private collection of memories.

The journey felt long and strained, both forever conscious of the countdown to midnight. They passed through Taunton and Reading. They were both thinking the same thing. What would life be like after midnight? Would the guilt consume them and take over their relationships? Would they always think of the other when they made love to Adam and Zara? They had changed as lovers, evolved together. Where did that leave them with their life partners? Great uncertainty plagued their thoughts.

The tune of Firestarter by The Prodigy invaded the carriage. 'Shit.' Kai quickly rummaged in his bag.

He mouthed brother to Charlotte. She nodded in response.

'Hi Ed, you alright?' Kai turned away from Charlotte, got up and walked to the corridor.

Charlotte tried to listen but could only make out vague mumbles.

Kai came back. 'Edgar just wanted to make sure the train was running on time for him to collect me.'

'Okay.'

Finally, the train pulled into Paddington Station. They stood up, kissed each other on the cheek and walked out on to the platform with their bags.

Kai found Ed first. They hugged each other.

'Zara is waiting for you, the kids tried staying up but are now all asleep. As you may have guessed, Chloe stayed up the longest.' Ed laughed.

Kai and Charlotte stared at each other as long as they dared. Adam found Charlotte and gave her a hug and a kiss. As she turned away a tear rolled down her cheek.

'Beef stew and dumplings are in the slow cooker if you're hungry,' said Adam cheerfully.

Charlotte mumbled thanks and lost sight of Kai in the crowd.

# TADPOLE

A black splodge in an egg mass, all big and small,
Bunched in together, constrained in one ball.
They have no minds, feelings, or sense
Just function of being, while they are close and intense.

They grow a tail, like a wriggly worm!
Not much movement, just a tiny squirm.
A slight attire of colour, to suit their new lives
Underwater is the only way they can survive.

Out pops their legs, first at the back
Donning more colour, now green from the black
Their eyes are defined, but still resembling fish
But they look more appealing, with a little more flourish.

Their front legs appear, classed a young frog
Still much to learn before they can leave the bog.
They need to know the ways and judge what is best
Before they are free to roam and join the rest.

Their transformation is complete, tadpoles are full-grown
Ready to leave their surroundings and all they have known.

Fourteen weeks is over, it's time to emerge.

The world is full of water and waits to be submerged.

# **<u>ANA</u>**

I looked over at Salvador and could not hold my disgust. He was staring and watching that whore, Gala like she was the most interesting thing in the whole of Spain. He used to look at me like that. Now he goes on and on about her form, the way her body is shaped, the curves, the lines. I was there from the start when the great Salvador Dali was just a teen and started painting. I helped him discover his gift, showed him how to grow. How can he dishonour me like this?

    I loved how gracefully mysterious he made me look on the canvas, just painted from behind in silhouette. He knew how to capture beauty. Should a sister be jealous of her brother's muse? It feels as if she has taken my place. I was the one Salvador studied, it made me feel special. Now the ungrateful soul has replaced me with a woman who has only a taste of intrigue. He calls her unique. The last creatures I heard described as unique were featured in a travelling circus.

    It makes me so angry when I see her acting like that. Sitting so still. Motionless, no life inside her. No show of a beating heart, blood flowing through her veins, no character. Just a cold statue against a wall no one wants to visit. I am sure they are sleeping together. I wonder if she is that cold and motionless in bed? The lengths men go to just to keep their phallus amused. It makes me so mad and sick.

    She has no life lived; no obstacles overcome. I have lived, I have hidden pain, haunting pain that my brother saw and exposed to the world as the heartache of a love lost. Salvador escaped everything whilst I was the one arrested, tortured and held captive. I can hear myself scream, cry, beg for leniency, begging and praying for kindness or hope. I dreamed of a hero, like in the fairy tales Papa used to read to me when my bed was a sanctuary. My body was then unmarked and innocent. Not corrupted, its pureness was stolen without much thought or reason other than Neanderthal nature and conquest. I am a survivor, in the paintings and sketches from Salvador, he showed me as I was once seen, before the dishonourable men and their mindless ungodly fun.

    I was again fair. Delicate in a way I was pleasing, not as fragile as reality reveals. I needed to see myself that way. As a work of art. Now Gala and my kin have forsaken me, my brother's actions no different than the monsters who took me away. Both ruled by want and empty of compassion or grace.

    He has not seen me watching him, she can feel me there watching her. I study her form, her thin arms, her bitter face, her dark empty eyes, her thin lips that do not beg to be kissed but instead show the face of a mother's scorn. Her eyebrows have shape, but her hair is short, unwomanly, unfeminine. He cannot paint her as she is, she is too unsightly. He instead paints her in fantastical ways. With me, he always showed me as I was, his love cascaded from the brush.

Unfortunately, fantasy sells, and Salvador's interpretations of Gala earn pesetas. I bring him a little but not enough for a livelihood which is what he desires more than anything, except mass recognition. Maybe that is why she is here. She makes him interesting. I am boring Ana. Nothing amazing or different about me anymore, just familiar territory. The usual brush strokes he's already done many times before. I am not unusual enough to attract new criticism of Salvador's work.

    I wish it were untrue, but I must concede he displays her in a way that requires thought whereas the portrayals of myself require no imagination to see any pleasantness or refinement. It is obvious to all.

    Her eyes flicker toward me to steal a glance. It's not enough she has stolen his captivation. A smile flickers in the corner of her mouth. I look at Salvador, he is mixing paint and did not see it. She is enjoying herself and the attention. Soon, he will talk of marriage I am sure, and I will be forced to embrace her into my life or forgo my relationship with my brother. Salvador can be irritating with his views. Maybe I will not have to embrace her, forgoing my ungrateful brother could be appealing. It will not be long before he falls out with Aunty and Papa anyway with his ridiculous behaviour, neither of them is thrilled with his choice of muse and bedfellow, so it will only be a matter of time.

I am glad Mama is not here, she would not hear any cross words about Salvador's art. He was considered the master, the gifted child, whilst I am my father's daughter. I wonder if my original brother Salvador would be as ungrateful and unfeeling as this one. Although they look alike, my guess is the original would be a bit more thoughtful and considerate and wouldn't be playing my ungrateful brother's role of a tortured artist with a surreal soul. How has Salvador suffered? I was the one accused of espionage and taken away. For my dreams to haunt me.

My only release is the movement and creation of words to express my shame and tormented soul. We both lost Mama, sure Salvador worshipped her more than I, but I still loved her, and I seek out her affection many times in a night.

I suppose he will always be tormented by our brother, the original. A life not lived has stolen treasures concocted by all who knew them. Even when taken as a babe, the aspirations of a future never met weigh heavily on those who grieve around them. Awareness of opportunities lost, drive over-compensation. I never saw Salvador-the-original take a breath, but I feel the love of a sibling for his being. I wish we knew each other, now he will always be perfect.

A life unlived means mistakes have never been made, no bad decisions have been taken, no hurt caused by impulse or bad habit. In many ways, we are worshipping an ideal. A mirage. I have no doubt he would have hated Gala. He would find her intolerable. He would have rescued me, given me hope and nurtured me when I returned home. He would have imparted peace, composure, and tranquillity during Mama's passing. He would have shown Salvador I was still worthy of the stroke of his brush. And deserved his time.

Alas, he is not here. All I can do is watch Gala and my brother in silence, knowing she believes she has won and taken my place. I try and convince myself I can never be replaced, whilst ignoring it has already happened and I am powerless to stop it. I have been reduced into a spectator. No longer a contribution to my brother's wild surrealistic creations. Sometimes I wish time would melt away and Gala was no longer an elephant stomping through our world but a beautiful swan, graceful and elegant. Maybe then I might like her, and we could be swans together. We could waste time and pretend we are tigers flying through the clouds in a dream.

I must become free. I have a mind, I have intellect. Intelligence without ambition is akin to a bird without wings. Maybe the time has come for me to fly.

# **A JOURNEY OF DEATH AND LIFE**

Day 1
I am sitting here in disbelief. Numb. Flummoxed. How could this happen? I only saw her eight days ago. This only happens to other people. I forget how to talk. I don't feel connected to anything.

I look out the window. Everyone in the outside world is acting so normal. How can they carry on? The world has fallen apart, my life is destroyed. An hour ago, I was screaming, my body clenched in a ball as tight as I could make it, lying on the floor.

I try to sip from my glass, my hand is shaking. I find my glass is empty. I need more whiskey.

Day 2
The family have arrived. Everyone is trying not to cry and are fussing around me and my mum. I want to tell them to go away, but their presence is a comfort. Everything is so confusing; I feel so conflicted. I can hear talking about mundane things that don't matter. WHO CARES!!!! Is screaming inside my head but on the outside I am silent.

I am still screaming inside. Make this go away, I want to tell them. Make it not true.
I need more whiskey. Arrangements are made, I am being told but I quickly forget what is said.

Day 3
Mum calls me. The coroner has been in touch. Cause of death is lack of oxygen to her heart. Congestive heart failure.

She is dead. The cause does not matter. All I care about is that it was quick, and she did not suffer. My mum tells me we can see her from tomorrow. She is desperate to be near her. I tell my mum I cannot bring myself to go. I am petrified at what I will find.

My mum turns up at my flat, she says she told me yesterday to expect her at 9am. I have no recollection of this at all. She picks me up and takes me to the funeral directors. I leave her to decide everything, I cannot imagine what she is going through. Her strength.

'You choose the music,' she tells me. 'You knew her best.'

I cannot hold a single thought in my head. It feels like I am visiting in an alien world where nothing makes sense. People seem to expect me to do something, but I don't know what it is, or what I am supposed to do. I want to leave this alien world and go back to the one I know, where she is still here.

The date is set. In 11 days, we will bury my sister.

Day 14

I am like a robot. I look down surprised that I got dressed. I don't remember doing so. The vicar talks, I cannot take anything in or concentrate. My partner holds my hand.

'32, it's no age.' 'Nice day. At least the weather stayed dry.' I hear these words again and again from relatives I have not seen since being a kid. People talk to me, but I can only nod.

I can see the coffin. Once I find it, I cannot move my gaze.

Sunflowers cover the casket. Each with a folded-up memory attached with string to its stem.

Leaving the room after the service is the hardest thing I have to do. This is the last time I will physically be with her. The funeral directors force me to leave. It is busy for them today.

Day 67

I AM FULL OF RAGE! I grab my childhood teddy bear and repeatedly pound it to the floor. I scream louder and louder, not caring who hears. WHY HER!?! WHY!?!

Day 112
The woman sits opposite me patiently. I cry quietly. I have already forgotten her name. I am waiting, hoping she will magic the hurt away. I need her to rescue me. Tell me a trick to make it all disappear. To give me back my memory, my love of reading, my smile. She gives me her card and tells me to call her when I am ready to talk. I smile and thank her. When she leaves, I am relieved.

Day 145
It is my partner's birthday. I have forgotten. I see the calendar as I make my morning coffee. I abandon the coffee and rush to the supermarket and get him two CDs, a bottle of whiskey and some doughnuts. I can't remember which ones he likes. I grab the first ones to hand.

He is awake when I return home, worried about where I went. We get drunk that evening and make love. Partly because I feel guilty, partly to feel normal. Neither work.

Day 173
Christmas Day. I am going through the motions and trying to make sure we have a good day. I stop at one glass of wine although I want more. I sit on the bed with only quiet surrounding me. They are all behind the door. I know everyone is watching, waiting for me to settle on the new person I must become. I do not recognise my old life. There will forever be a part of myself that is lost, I cannot go back. I must find an adaptation of myself that I am comfortable with. Someone who can be happy, at least for a little while.

Day 289
Her birthday. One of the many she will never see. I go through her old messages on my phone. I pretend she is just a call away. That she is celebrating abroad which is why I

can't be near her.

My counsellor calls to finalise an appointment. I don't tell her about today. My thoughts have been full of so much isolation and sadness. I always end up apologising after each session for being so negative.

I do not tell her I am pregnant. My partner suggested the baby comes from my sister. To remind us there is still a lot of our lives left to live, new experiences to be had. But I am scared. What if I lose my baby and my sister?

I am scared that I will feel no attachment to my baby. I am finding it so hard to be close to others, to care about anything. What if I project these feelings and negativity on to my child?

My partner is helping by writing times of when and what to eat, as my memory is terrible now. I'm scared to tell my mum.

Day 365
I am standing with my family. Everyone is talking about how much they miss and love my sister. I am holding hands with the woman who is a pale reflection of the person my mother used to be. Silently the tears fall down her cheeks as she tries to speak. My mum is moving next month so she can be closer to us and the baby.

A gentle wind flows through me and blows my hair away from my nose. I place my hands over my stomach and close my eyes. The glow of the sun warms my face.

We are each holding a silver balloon. My mum squeezes my hand. My turn to speak.
'I love you, Chloe. I will never forget you.' I know it will be a long time before I stop feeling so empty. But I do also know there is a life waiting for me.

'Goodbye,' I whisper.

I will never take a moment without appreciation. I am grateful for my life and I will make my sister proud.

As I say the words, I unclench my fist and let go of the pink ribbon. The balloon floats up to the heavens. I watch it rise, glance at my mum, and faintly smile. I look up and my balloon is gone. Vanished when I wasn't looking, never to be seen or held again.

I can hear footsteps behind me as my partner places his hand over mine. We look at each other. He pulls me close and kisses my head. Without a word, we turn around and walk away.

# STAR WARS

Few films can be recognised around the world using just one sentence. But as soon as you hear or see *A long time ago in a galaxy far far away...* You know that film is Star Wars. It is arguably the most iconic line in movie history. But what makes Star Wars so special? Of course, there are the themes of good versus evil, dark vs light, God vs Satan, but a big part of the fascination is down to one man and his vision.

Before a frame was filmed or cut, George Lucas knew what he was doing. The whole saga was in his head, Episodes 4-6. Wait 20 years, release episodes 1-3. And he kept to his plan despite huge pressure from everyone due to the phenomenal success and mania that followed *A New Hope*'s release.

Everything was his creation. The idea was heavily ridiculed, even by the cast, but the imagination and determination of one man defies belief. The lightsabers alone are incredible, every fan no matter their age has played with one, done that distinctive noise, had fights with their friends and dreamed of owning one for real.

The look and concept were clear in George Lucas's mind from the beginning, he knew exactly what he wanted. And the worlds and galaxies are so intricate, each one with its own species and history, not to mention monsters!

Every planet is beautifully designed, and so different from the others. In Tatooine, it is mostly sand with two suns. Quite a sparse population inhabit with most residents needing moisture farms to survive. The heat means it has no natural plants at all, but of course the planet is essential for the Star Wars story. Many will know Luke Skywalker comes from Tatooine, as does his father Anakin. It is through the pod race in Tatooine that we see Anakin's remarkable skills as a pilot from such a young age. It is also where his journey to the dark side begins, changing his path towards becoming the iconic Darth Vader.

Jabba the Hutt, weighing a massive 1,358kg enslaves Leia at his palace on the sand planet. And it also sets the scene where the heavyweight gangster and crime lord ends up meeting his demise. Throughout the saga, Jabba is a central character to events. From the bounty on Han Solo's head, to running the pod races where Anakin grabs the attention of the Jedi Knights visiting that day.

It is not just big crime lords that you need to watch out for in Tatooine. Jawas are master scavengers. Just one metre tall and heavy cloaked, they are the first on the scene of any crash site. They also have an untrustworthy reputation as a result from swindling and selling faulty droids to the locals.

Tusken Raiders are a nasty version of the Jawas, looking vicious in their unpleasant masks. They have a firm belief the land is theirs along with every moisture farm, which they will attack if they find it.

What these small descriptions show is how vast and complex each world is. From the luxurious glamour of Cloud City to the volcanic lava infested Mustafar, to the green paradise and lakes of Naboo, the ice of unforgiving Hoth, and the forest home of Ewoks, Endor. So many details with so much imagination.

But it isn't just the worlds, the characters in Star Wars are exquisite. You have the handsome smuggler who is a little bit cheeky, the princess who is beautiful but fiercely independent, to the Wookie who on paper should be scary. Masses of hair from head to toe, and a giant at 2.3m tall. Yet he is so loveable, although he never says a word we can understand!

Never have pieces of metal been so loved as R2-D2, BB-8 or C-3PO, or villains been as cool as Darth Maul (that fantastic duel with his double lightsaber was outstanding) or General Grievous who put everyone to shame by fighting with four lightsabers at once! Luke is the ultimate humble farm boy on a quest, and you have the character the original six movies were all about: Anakin Skywalker.

I could write a whole book on Anakin Skywalker. The character is so complex yet so relatable and he teaches us such a valuable lesson.

One of the reasons the Star Wars saga was released out of numerical order was because George Lucas wanted us invested in Darth Vader. He wanted us to see him as the unforgiving, powerful, dangerous enemy so when we learnt that he was Luke's father it would have the ultimate impact. The hero was the son of his nemesis.

In that incredible moment when Darth Vader brought balance to the force, we understood there was good within him and we wanted to see how he became as evil as he did. This left us desperate to see the first three films to find out.

When we were finally allowed to go back to the beginning, we were able to see Anakin as a boy. We found out little details such as he was the creator of the beloved C-3PO, that Luke inherited his pilot skills from his dad, and just how powerful the force was within him. We see him as a young man, we watch as he falls in love with Luke and Leia's mother (an act forbidden to a Jedi as it can lead to dark traits such as jealousy and loss), knowing it will end in tragedy. And how he became an Apprentice to the much-revered Obi-Wan Kenobi. We are invested in their relationship from the beginning, learning how it all ended in that fateful duel in *A New Hope*. Of course, this left just the final stage.

Everyone wanted to see Anakin's journey reach full darkness and go full circle and as a result, Revenge of the Sith took more than half a billion dollars. The films all together have made an astonishing $9.4 billion worldwide and that's not including any merchandise.

I did say Anakin Skywalker teaches us a valuable lesson.

Anakin had gone from a sweet talented little boy to a monster who took many lives including Jedi knights and children. He had reached the pits of despair, the lowest a human could ever go, all he had was hatred and anger. Yet although it seemed all hope was lost, he ended up saving the Galaxy by bringing peace and balance, saving so many lives.

Luke always believed in his father; he never gave up. There is always someone who believes in you. It is never too late to make a difference or do the right thing, everyone has the power to do so, you just need to be brave enough to do it.

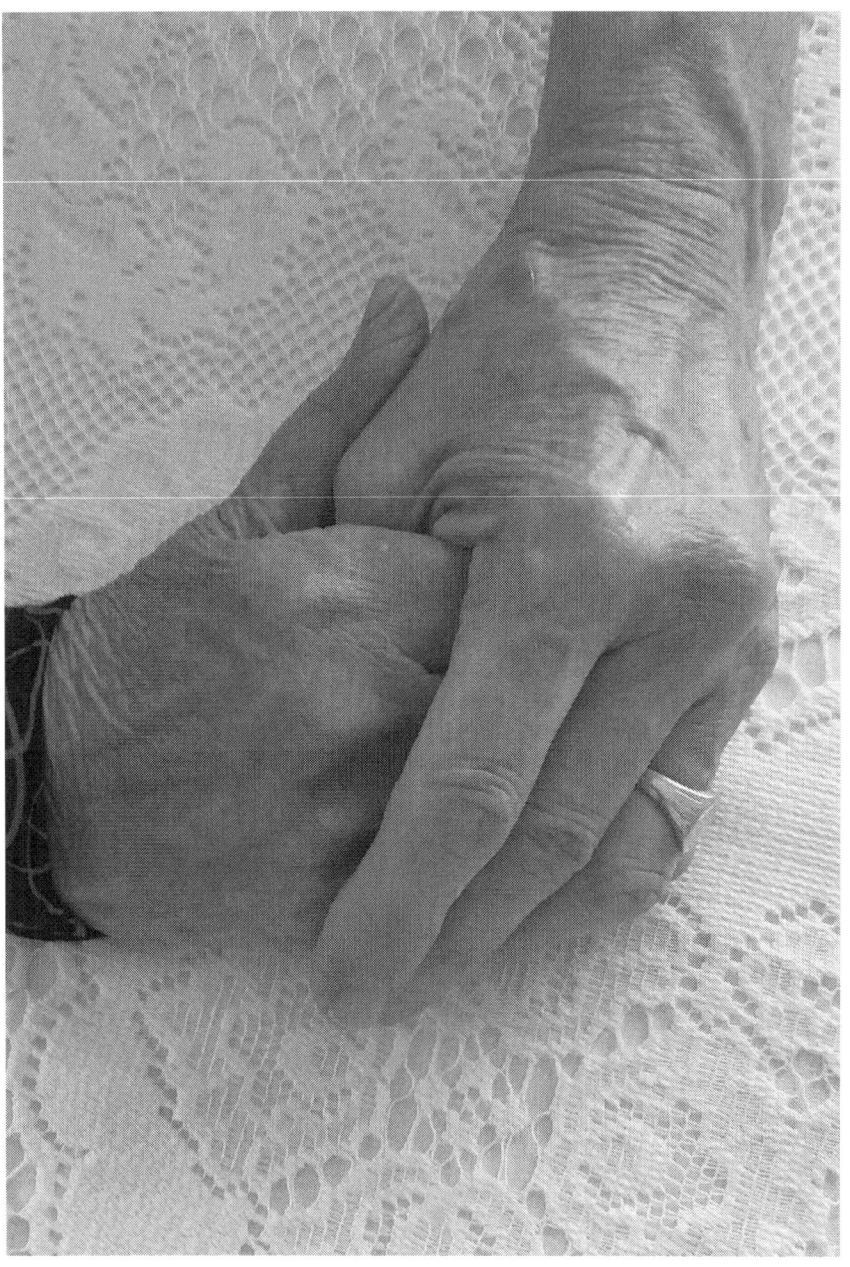

# WILLY AND GERT

This is the story of Willy and Gert
Of their life together
The best and the worst.

They met at school,
On the first day
When Willy tagged her
And Gert ran away.

Willy became her boyfriend,
They held each other's hand.
He sat next to Gert in class
She played recorder in the school band.

The teens kicked in,
They kissed each other more.
Plans began to get made
Of the future they saw.

Gert was good with words,
She became a secretary.
Willy was more physical,

And joined the Military.

Willy and Gert got engaged
In six months, they would say 'I do'.
But Willy got called away
At the break of World War Two.

Gert had to change her job
She began work in a factory.
Whilst Willy faced bombs and gas
In a land across the sea.

Letters were their salvation
Their messages from home.
So, when the darkness fell
They didn't feel so alone.

A photo of Gert was taped to Willy's bed
And Willy on the post of Gert's.
They kissed it goodnight before every sleep
And hid how much it hurt.

Letters ceased without warning,
Word could not get through.
Families got more and more worried

But there was nothing they could do.

Casualties escalated every day,
Bombs invaded their town.
Friends and work-friends were lost,
Buildings and ash rained down.

Gert never lost hope,
Her wedding day would come.
Willy would hold her again in his arms,
Cover her in kisses and love.

Then one Thursday afternoon
Willy was coming home.
He lost an arm and some comrades
After the bombs had blown.

Willy went to his mum and dads
Not knowing what to expect.
When Gert found he was not whole
That her beloved was not perfect.

At first, he could not see her,
He was more scared than in the war.
That she could no longer love him,

She was who he was fighting for.


In the end, they met by chance,

Walking down the road.

Gert immediately embraced him,

Love and joy were all she showed.


What a glorious day for them both,

After so much time away.

Deciding there would be no more waiting,

They were married the next day.


Willy and Gert shared a home,

Willy became a clerk.

Gert became a mother of four,

And an artist, along with her housework.


The years passed, the children grew,

They loved more than ever.

But then Willy became sick,

And began to forget their moments together.


People disappeared slowly,

As Willy's mind got worse.

He relied on his wife more than ever,

Gert became his nurse.

But they could not be parted,
For a night or a day.
One day he asked, 'Who are you?'
As his memories slipped away.

Gert's body was now failing,
They entered a hospice as one.
A room shared together,
With a window to watch the dawn.

One morning, Willy would not wake.
Gert followed him four minutes later.
At their bedside, their family grieved pain and loss,
Of Willy and Gert, and their eighty years together.

# **THE ABSENTEE**

There is a couple that I know

Where others do not see what's beyond the show.

The mum and dad are both on the dole

They have four kids, a packed schedule.

Preschool, nursery, primary school…

A lot to juggle, so much to do.

The mum drops the kids off at the gates

They are always on time, never late.

But because its only mum they see,

They consider the dad an absentee.

Yet, he cleans, organises, and feeds the mouths

The mum just watches him around the house.

He is restless, eager to work

But he can't find a job, he does nothing but look.

He gets all four kids dressed and out the door,

And once they're gone, he starts on the chores.

Yet, because this is the part other parents do not see,

They consider him an absentee.

He does the homework, bedtimes, and night calls.

He bandages them up whenever they fall.

This dad is priceless, he dotes, and never falters

I love this dad; he's inspirational. I am his daughter.

## **IN THE HANDS OF THE GODS**

Today was the day of reckoning for Planet Earth. Gaea, Mother Earth, sat on her throne and rubbed her neck.

'Perses, Athena, you are my council. What is my future? Will I become childless?' Gaea said.

Perses, a giant of a man stepped forward, 'Mother Gaea. I think we have passed the point of no return. The earth is dying. People are doing nothing. All hope is lost.'

'Mother Gaea if I may,' Athena interjected, 'I have faith in humanity.' She took off her golden helmet and pulled it free of her long aureate hair. 'Perses, like me, you believe in the need for destruction but also for peace. Allow me a few moments and I will prove there is hope.'

'Very well Athena.' Perses replied. 'Proceed.'

Athena walked over to a pool of water and took off the gilded ornate shield that hung on her back. She laid the shield on the ground, cupped her hands in the water and poured it into the inside of the armour. Athena held it with both hands, lifted it carefully and swirled the water inside.

She took it over to Gaea and Perses. She placed the shield down on the stone floor and spun the water with her finger.

An image appeared. A sea. And then two small parachutes.

'Fifty years ago, the United States of America was in the middle of a terrible war. It lasted almost twenty years from beginning to end. Amongst all the hostilities and tragedy, there was a lot of hope for three people. Look closer, what do we see?'

Athena dipped the tip of her finger in the surface of the water. It rippled and a vision of people kneeling came into focus.

'What is happening?' asked Perses.

'They are praying. 10,000 people are praying in Italy for the safe return of three men. Ten times that are praying in India. People around the world are watching television and pleading to God for three astronauts to make it home safe. These astronauts are strangers to these people. They failed their mission, but they united the world amidst great conflict and suffering.'

'Did they make it home?' asked Gaea.

'Yes, the astronauts of Apollo 13 made it home. Eleos intervened and answered their prayers,' said Athena. 'But it was the people who made him stand up and take notice.'

'Athena, one example from 50 years ago does not prove a point.'

'I understand that, Perses. Let me go back another fifty years to 1920.'

'What's special about 1920?' Perses asked.

'The League of Nations was formed.' replied Athena.

'The what?'

'The League of Nations. Countries around the world came together as one for World Peace.'

'Go back another fifty,' Perses said. 'If humanity is as great as you believe, show us another time now.'

'Okay, look here.' Athena dipped her finger once again in the water. A family appeared. They wore clothes with holes and were sharing broth and a loaf of bread. The mother sat sewing in the corner. 'This family give every penny they have to a landlord who lives hundreds of miles away in a large house in London. They have no rights. The mother feeds the children and husband but not herself. She has not eaten in days.'

'Why not the husband?' asked Gaea.

'He needs his strength to work the land, to get money to pay increasing rent prices,' said Athena sadly. 'There are families like this all over Ireland until William Gladstone decided to do something and he changed the law. He gave the tenants more rights. It didn't solve the problem, but he started to try and change things.'

Athena put her finger in the water again. The ripples revealed a woman on the street. 'This woman was thrown out of her home by her husband who had an affair and moved his lover inside afterwards. She became homeless. Her home was left by her parents, and her husband took every penny she earnt and spent on his mistress.'

'I think that shows the cruel side of humanity,' Perses smirked.

'An act was passed, giving women rights to hold onto their property and money for those who were married after 1870. When she married again three years later, she was safe in the knowledge that what she earnt and worked for was hers, and hers alone.'

'What about the women already married?' asked Gaea.

Athena looked to the water. 'They waited twelve years for it to become law for everyone.' She looked at Gaea. 'In both cases, the problem was not solved straight away, but they saw the obstacles people faced and started to try to change things. Sometimes change takes time and is drawn out. It may be difficult to see, especially in crisis but it does happen.'

'Interesting point. Please keep going Athena.' said Gaea.

Athena nodded. 'Let's go back another fifty years.' She touched the water with her finger and ripples revealed a sea. 'This is Portloe in Cornwall.'

Perses peered in to look at the shield water. 'Is it night?'

'Very early in the morning.'

Within the water, there was an image of boats and people on a beach.

'What's happening?' asked Gaea.

'The Ship Idea has crashed on the cliffs of Nare head. The village of Portloe sent men from their homes to help look for survivors. The villagers that can help are on the beach.'

'Do they know people from the ship?' Perses asked.

She jerked her head to look at him. 'No,' replied Athena.

Perses tilted his body to look closer. 'Then, why?'

'There were people on the ship.' Athena answered watching him. 'They need to make sure they have done everything possible to make sure they are safe.'

'Were there any survivors?' Gaea asked.

'No. No one was ever found.'

'Then...'

'They searched for eight hours. Some ten, ' interrupted Athena. 'Even when the situation seemed hopeless, they kept trying. They wanted to know they had done everything in their power to save them.'

Gaea and Perses stared at the water in silence.

'I will go back another fifty years.' Athena created the ripples with her finger. The liquid settled to show a thin tiny woman feeding a handful of rice to her small child.

'This is a mother in Birbhum in India. She is dying of starvation but no matter how badly she wants food, she gives every grain of her small handful of rice to her six-year-old son. She doesn't know when they will get more, and she cannot bring herself to take anything he will need to survive. Millions of mothers made the same sacrifice and gave their lives for the sake of their children.'

A tear ran down the cheek of Gaea, Mother Earth. She remembered the famine. It still hurt her now.

'I could go back fifty years again and again and show you different people from around the world, but I feel like 250 years has proven my point. You are scared for your world Mother Gaea, but I can see you know there is hope. Humanity has great empathy and desire for love and peace. They come together and carry on fighting for the future and each other. Sometimes changes will be small, but every effort counts and together they can shape the future and save your wonderful creation. Life can challenge humanity but when they come together as one, they are an incredible force. Believe in humanity. Believe in hope.'

'Thank you, Athena. When I created Earth, it was a paradise, an array of greens and blues containing so much life. It has given me so much pleasure to watch humans evolve and embrace the natural splendours I set out for them. However, it has also given a great ache in my heart when I see the reason for my existence abused and uncared for. Creatures faded away from memory and existence. Based on what you have shown me there is reason to have faith, and the people below present great promise. I will trust and follow your guidance. Perses?'

'I agree, Mother Gaea. Let's hope the human race realises the power they hold in their hands. They live in a beautiful world. Its survival could be their ultimate legacy.'

# **BE CAREFUL WHAT YOU SEARCH FOR**

The general public hated Cedric Bluth. The whole country was in a shambles, and the only reason Cedric got the job of Prime Minister was that no one else wanted it. He had always dreamed of reaching the top, and no matter how short his term was, Cedric knew he would always be remembered. Perhaps not in the way he wished, but still remembered. Even if it was just as an answer on Pointless, his favourite show. He felt he would now go down in history, joining the long line of Prime Ministers before him.

The problem was that, since he took office, nothing was going right, or at all how he imagined. His audience with the Queen had been a disaster. He thought he would ask for a selfie with her and tweet it to become popular with the young folk. Instead, the Queen threatened to shove his phone up his backside if he didn't put it away, and a Corgi peed on his trouser leg. He needed to get the public onside but desperately needed an idea.

Then, on Wednesday afternoon, the idea came. Everyone hated internet trolls, he would fish them out and expose them; and then have them arrested under a new law he could put through parliament. Incredibly pleased with himself, Cedric pressed the button on the intercom,

'Can you come in here number two?'

A small man came into the room, 'What can I do for you, Sir?'

'Ah, number two…'

'My name is Thomas, Sir.'

Cedric waved his arm as he brushed the last comment away, 'Very good, number two. I want everyone's internet searches in the UK.'

'Excuse me, Sir?'

'Don't worry number 2, I didn't hear it. Everyone's searches. On google and whatnot.'

'There are privacy laws, Sir.'

Cedric crossed his arms and puffed out his chest, 'How come the police can do it then?'

'Well, if they suspect someone...'

'I suspect everybody!' Cedric interrupted, flinging his arms around in the air. 'Even you, number two!' he exclaimed as he pointed at Thomas. 'And I am head of the country! I make the laws! Get to work and flush those blighters out!'

Having no idea who 'those blighters' were, Thomas just replied 'Right-O.' and walked backwards out of the Prime Minister's office.

Cedric walked to his desk and put his feet up on important papers, happy with his days' work. A surveillance photo was stuck to the bottom of his shoe. Irritated, Cedric picked it off and flicked it away letting it float to the floor.

The following Tuesday morning, Thomas knocked on the Prime Ministers door with an extreme amount of paper,

'Here are the google searches as you requested, Prime Minister.'

Cedric Bluth, who was amid putting together a relief order to Africa threw it to the ground with a big grin. He clapped his hands, bounced in his chair, and his feet drummed on the carpet in celebration of his brilliant idea coming to fruition.

'So, this is the whole of the country is it number two?'

'Again, my name is Thomas. Well, it's 5% of the UK Population Sir.'

Cedric frowned. 'What? But I asked for everyone.'

'Well, there are a lot of us, Sir.'

'Uh-huh. Well, any initial observations?'

'Well Sir, a lot of ailment searching, and people asking for instructions on how to floss dance.'

'What is that? A dentistry term?'

Thomas laughed heartily and snorted before he could control himself, 'Very good. Sir.'

Cedric looked at him with pity. He had suspected for the last month, he was some kind of equal opportunity employment due to a mental disability.

'What else number two?'

Thomas shook his head to gain professionalism and continued, 'Keanu Reeves Memes are popular as are Happy birthday ones. There's a lot of Is Andrew Scott gay?'

Cedric looked at Thomas. 'Who is Andrew Scott?'

'He is the hot priest in Fleabag, Sir,'

'Where is Fleabag? Have we been there? Never mind. Arrange a visit there for the end of the year. We may be missing out on a few votes.'

Before Thomas could respond, the Prime Minister spoke again, 'come on, number two! Where's the dirty stuff? You know! The stuff that can get people in trouble.'

Thomas walked over to the papers for inspiration. 'Ok Sir. We had, is it cheating if I fantasise about the postman? How do I get my husband to tidy up his pubic hair? Am I lesbian if I lust after Kim Kardashian's bottom? Any of those Sir?'

Cedric didn't react.

Thomas looked in desperation, 'can you make poison from egg whites? Can you die from undercooked chicken? How do I get paid for sexual favours?'

Cedric tried to look where Thomas was reading, 'do we have a lot of strippers and prostitutes in the UK?'

'All of those are your wife's searches, Sir,' said Thomas, a little too happily.

Cedric stared at Thomas intently. 'Just read from the top, and I'll tell you when I know what I'm looking for.'

'Are you sure Sir?'

'Definitely.'

Thomas's eyes lit with mischief, 'Right-O. Dwarfs threesome with baguette. Women dressed as pigs with cucumbers. You do like your food, Sir.'

'They are not mine!' Cedric protested, pulling at his shirt collar.

'Well, you did say start from the top Sir, and that you wanted everybody. But if you are sure you didn't search for those things Sir, then we may have a serious security breach which would mean a meeting immediately with the Head of Defence. Would you like me to arrange that for you, Sir?'

Cedric wiped his hands on his trousers. This was not going as planned. 'That's okay.'

Thomas smirked. 'Bacon salad baguette for lunch today Sir?'

Cedric flicked his gaze violently to Thomas, 'Shut up. No one likes a smart-arse number two. Where's yours?'

Thomas flicked through some papers until he came to page forty-three. 'Here we are Sir.'

Cedric stood beside him and read the report. 'What the hell is Quilting World?'

Thomas raised his head and lifted his chin, 'I do needlework, Sir. I find it relaxing.'

'Uh-huh.' Cedric flicked through the papers, noisily. 'There's a lot of people asking if I'm dead.'

'Yes Sir, you and Brian Blessed.'

'Is Brian Blessed dead?'

'I don't think so, Sir.'

Cedric let out a big sigh. He couldn't be bothered to look through all this now. The troll thing might be a nonstarter. 'Don't worry about the rest of the UK number two.'

Thomas smiled, 'very good Sir. Anything else Sir?'

'Yes. Change our postman.'

'Very good Sir.' confirmed Thomas as he stepped out the office.


Cedric pushed the papers to the floor for the cleaner and turned on his computer. He then rang his tech guy to find out how to delete his history.

One of the biggest dreams when I've imaged myself as an author was writing in Paris, by a window. For my 40th Birthday, we went away for three days to go Disneyland Paris (I am a massive Disney fan, we were ticking off the bucket list). I was staying in a Parisian chalet with my family and on the morning of my birthday, I sat out on the veranda with my netbook surrounded by nature and typed.

    I did an exercise I often do to get my brain warmed up where you just describe everything around you. This is my prose from that moment. I still pinch myself I got to do this, and it remains one of the greatest memories I look back on fondly.

```
I sit here in Paris on the morning of my
40th birthday. An aspiration throughout my
writer's journey, the feeling of a dream
fulfilled warms my body and soul. I am eager
```

to note everything, so I will not forget a single second or layer of my memory of this moment. I let my fingers type as I close my eyes and let the world inspire me with its creations and evolutions only available to me at this precise time and location. Like so many other seconds in our lives, this will never be available to me again.

Darkness surrounds me, the light from my laptop is my guide to the words that form in my head. The world is yet to wake up, it is quiet. The moon glows brightly and I am surrounded by the night sky. Stars twinkle above my head as aeroplanes fly passengers to new worlds from a faraway distance. The moon is setting, allowing the world a new day. The sun is yet to show life on earth, unearthing the beauty nature can behold.

Classical music plays in the distance and geese wake, chattering about the day ahead.

The sunrise is coming. It is eager to arrive.

I hold the mug of hot coffee and wrap my hands around it lovingly, taking comfort from its heat and satisfying my need for caffeine. I can hear my children playing. Heated words. But I am reluctant to leave my new Utopia.

The clouds boast a blissful pink. The sky is more purple now, the geese seem to have said all they have to say. The music has stopped. I hear water, and now the light has come, I can see a bridge presides over a river. The children have gone quiet. It's as if the world waits for that wondrous moment when the sun will emerge and mark a new beginning.

I embrace my nirvana with gratitude. Tomorrow will change, I will not be here, neither will my little travel blue netbook. Some other fortunate soul will have the chance to experience their dreams becoming a reality or it will pass them by without them sparing it a thought or action. A moment of reflection to embrace nature and appreciate time made just for them.

So, I will type, etching this feeling into my brain so I never forget. Tapping my keys silently so I do not disturb the serenity of this tranquil place.

Parisians and travellers watched in terror, witnesses of the night when a sacred ground became immersed in a blazing inferno.

They cried, 'WE ARE HELPLESS! THERE IS NOTHING WE CAN DO!'

They were wrong.

Fire teams battled together and diminished the flames. A brave priest risked his life to save the crown of thorns and other priceless relics. Treasures that would otherwise be lost in history and fables, never to be seen again. Mortal men came together and fought for their beloved haven of worship and faith.

They wept in despair as the spire fell, 'IT WILL ALL BE GONE!'

They were wrong.

850 years aged, the glass windows and bell towers remained. Defying nature, unwavering against the peril surrounding them. The next morning light shone on the unbroken altar and lit up the gold cross. A miracle, a message from heaven. This medieval sanctuary is protected. It is powerful and strong. There is always hope.

People type on the internet around the world, 'IT'S JUST A BUILDING.'

They are wrong.

Notre Dame means beauty. Notre Dame means elegance. Visitors up to that moment, based city breaks to Paris so they could fulfil a life's dream and see its legendary beauty. The gothic divine structure that inspired books and films.

Notre Dame looked after its people. Sightseers empathised with the beggar woman crouched beside the arch and she ate that day thanks to the allure and splendour of the Cathedral. Themed hotels created jobs for locals, a small café owner opposite the man-made wonder lived independently thanks to Notre Dame. Customers flocked to newsagents, buses, trains, and the Metro. Writers created, artists became inspired by the beauty and structure of Notre Dame. Hope was given to the lost, comfort was given to those who grieved, a celestial presence was felt by those who believed. The gargoyles watched over the city of Paris with elegance and grace.

Work has only begun to save what was not smothered by the blaze, whispered secrets have been swallowed by the flames, but worshippers will always remember the joy and grandeur of the magnificent structure before the inferno. Photographs will be treasured, the statues removed for renovation will always be looked upon with gratitude.

The Cathedral will be rebuilt, but we will never forget the day the world shed a tear and mourned for the heart of Paris. The magnificent Notre Dame.

# **NOT JUST OLD- SUPER OLD!**

Freddie got off his bike outside the large metal gates and pressed the buzzer.

BUZZ!!!! 'Metrogoth Retirement Home?'

'Hi, I'm Freddie Rabbit. I'm here to volunteer for my Boy Scouts helping badge.'

'Oh yes. Please come in.'

BUZZ! The gates started to open. Freddie led his bike inside. The building was the biggest he had ever seen. The entranceway was between two stone pillars and had a large wooden door. Freddie turned and watched as the gates closed behind him.

It's probably safe to leave the bike he thought. He left it against the wall, next to the big door. Freddie pushed against the handle, but it wouldn't budge. Behind, he heard a clip-clap and the sound of bolts being released.

It swung open to reveal a lady with blonde hair, 'hi, Freddie. Your uncle told us to expect you. Please come in.'

Freddie walked inside to a little hall and a massive room. The ceiling was a big circle of glass showcasing bright blue sky with very few clouds. It was cool.

'I'm Valerie,' the blonde lady said as she held out her hand. 'Let me show you around.'

She led him on a tour of the place which was just a load of rooms. The garden was big, plenty of space to kick a football about.

'So, Boy Scouts huh?' she said as they walked. 'I used to be a Girl Scout myself.'

Freddie wondered why she thought he'd be interested. Girl Scouts was the girly version of his Scout troupe, only more fluffy and boring.

As they walked around, Freddie looked at the old people in the home. They were all old, but there was something about them. They seemed cool and all, but different somehow.

Freddie wondered what he would have to do whilst he was here. He enjoyed Boy Scouts, but this seemed like a lot of trouble for one badge. He wouldn't have bothered but his mum said that helping people was the most important badge of all. Freddie liked making her happy.

'It's coming on to lunchtime, I hate to put you in the deep end. But would you like to help out with that?' Valerie smiled.

Freddie shrugged, 'sure. No problem.'

They entered a room where there were lots of tables and it smelt of musk.

'What do you want me to do?' asked Freddie.

'Just help anyone who needs it and talk to them. They love a new face,' Valerie answered.

'Cool.'

Freddie stepped forward and moved around a little, someone dropped a fork. He picked it up and went to the cutlery tray on the side of the room to get them a clean one. Valerie watched him, smiled, and left the room.

'Thank you, Son,' they said when he returned with the new fork.

He wandered about and saw a table with just a couple of old guys sat on it. 'Would you mind if I sat down?'

The two guys looked at Freddie and smiled. One grin was much wider than the other.

'Of course not. Put it there, Sonny.' The wider smiler said with his hand outstretched.

Freddie shook his hand.

'BUZZ!' the man screamed and laughed hysterically.

'Don't mind him,' the other man said and turned to his friend. 'Trickster! I told you! It doesn't work anymore and you shouting Buzz doesn't scare anybody!'

The wide smiler looked theatrically sad.

Freddie shrugged, 'I was a little scared.'

The wide smile returned. 'Were you boy?' he started laughing again rather hysterically. 'See! Rodent Breath! I scared the boy!'

'Please, Trickster. No one must know my secret identity.'

'Bill, EVERYONE knows your secret identity! You're obvious!'

Now the other guy looked sad whilst the one known as Trickster just laughed.

Another old guy came and sat down.

'Mr Fandabbydoozy. How are you?'

'Don't call me that. I'm Richard Richards remember,' he signalled towards Freddie. 'We have company.'

To Freddie, it looked like he was trying not to move his lips but was failing miserably.

'Hello, son. I'm Richard.'

'Richards?' Freddie finished.

'Yes. Pleased to meet you,' he smiled and held out his hand. Freddie shook it.

'BUZZ!'

'Bit delayed there, Trickster,' the old man known as Rodent Breath aka Bill informed him.

'Yeah, I wasn't scared that time. Sorry,' said Freddie.

'Overkill,' said Trickster, 'always my problem.'

'Yeah, remember when you built that giant head of yourself to cover up your secret lair of goons?' Rodent breath said laughing, 'that was stupid.'

'Even I heard about that,' said Richard Richards as he joined in with the laughter, 'and I was in another universe!'

'I have a question,' said Freddie, 'why does everyone keep calling me 'Son'?'

'You are a young man, what else are we meant to call you?' replied Rodent Breath.

'Umm, well Freddie?'

'Freddie what?'

'Freddie Rabbit?'

'Oh no, that will never do. You need either a name like Freedman or your last name beginning with the same letter as your first. Like Freddie Fox,' informed Richard Richards.

'Why?' asked Freddie

'That's the rules,' said Rodent Breath.

'What rules?'

'The rules of being a superhero.'

Freddie protested, 'I'm not a superhero! I'm just a kid.'

'So was Firework,' said Richard.

'And my beloved Wren,' added Rodent Breath.

'Beloved is right.'

'Shut it, Trickster! Those rumours were never founded!'

'I know Rodent Breath! I started them!' He started laughing hysterically again.

'You bastard, Trickster! They followed us around for years. I ought to knock you to the ground!'

'Bill, please. Language,' said Richard Richards, 'the boy!'

Trickster sneered, 'careful Rodent Breath, the last time you picked a fight with me, you dislocated a hip!'

Rodent Breath and Trickster looked mean at each other. Then, without taking his eyes off him, Rodent breath stole his miniature bowl of rice pudding.

'Hey give that back! It's mine!'

Rodent Breath held it high. 'No. Not until you apologise!'

'Here have mine,' said Richard. 'Sorry, son. They are always like this.'

'No! I want mine, they put cinnamon in it just for me and he knows that! He's just being mean!'

'Mr Rodent Breath,' Freddie interjected. 'Maybe you should give it back to Mr Trickster, especially if they made it just for him. You seem like a nice man. I am sure he will say sorry if you do.'

'Okay,' Rodent Breath said and put the rice pudding back on the Tricksters tray. 'Just for the record though, my name isn't Rodent Breath. It's Bill.'

'Sorry, Mr Bill,' said Freddie.

'No problem.'

'Sorry Bill.' said Trickster.

'No problem.' said Bill.

'So, what did you mean when you said about superheroes?' Freddie asked.

'Oh, well, we all are. Superheroes I mean,' said Bill.

The Trickster did a loud cough.

'And Ummm...supervillains,' Bill added.

Trickster smiled, 'thank you.'

Bill smiled back, 'you're welcome.'

Freddie shuffled in his seat as he spoke, 'but you don't look like superheroes or supervillains. I mean, I'm a big comic book fan and they are all...'

Bill raised an eyebrow, 'young?'

Freddie looked down, 'yes. Sorry.'

Richard placed his hand on Freddie's shoulder, 'no offence taken. Well, everyone ages son. We were all heroes together and this is the only place that can take us.'

'Do you all have special powers?' asked Freddie.

'Not all. I had inventions,' said Bill.

'He means toys,' added Trickster.

Bill shot him a look. 'Inventions.'

'Where are all your inventions now?' asked Freddie.

Bill looked sad, 'I had to take them to be recycled.'

'Why?'

Bill looked awkward, 'well, it's a bit embarrassing.'

'What happened?' asked Freddie.

'Ooohhh can I tell him?' asked Trickster joyfully.

Bill shot him another look. 'No.'

'Oh, go on, I get so much pleasure from it!' The smile was wide again.

'They no longer make the right batteries.'

Trickster laughed manically.

Freddie leant closer. 'I'm sorry? All your toys ran on batteries?'

'They were inventions,' defended Bill. 'And it wasn't any batteries they were Super long extended charge batteries. But the green protestors came along and put a stop to them. Everything's solar now.'

Richard shook his head. 'It was a sad day.'

'Oh. I'm sorry. '

'Thanks, kid.'

Freddie turned to Richard, 'so, do you have special powers or were you an inventor like Mr Rodent Breath?'

'Bill,' corrected Bill.

'Sorry. Mr Bill.'

Bill turned to Trickster, 'you do realise the kid thinks that's my actual name now,' and Trickster laughed.

Richard ate a spoonful of potatoes, 'I elasticated my body.'

'Oh, that's cool.'

'Yeah, till he got arthritis, and a bad case of gout,' added Trickster.

'I am afraid it is true. I can no longer stretch.'

'Well, you can but it hurts,' laughed Bill.

Richard nodded, 'yep. Like hell.' They all laughed apart from Freddie.

Richard went on, 'my wife could go invisible.'

'Wow. That's really cool,' said Freddie cheerfully.

'Yeah,' said Richard. 'Then the visibility came in a shade of dusty pink, so she doesn't bother now. It used to be quite handy when you got peckish in the night or you wanted to steal a bit of the manager's secret stash of liquor for a birthday. But they see her coming now.'

Freddie looked around the dining hall. 'Where is she?'

Richard avoided his gaze. 'She's been confined to our room. It was my birthday last week and I fancied a tipple.'

Freddie nodded, 'so, is there anyone else who can do stuff?

Bill pointed, 'well, you see Kevin over there with the blue hair?'

Freddie looked, 'yeah.'

'He could teleport. That was useful,' said Bill. 'Unfortunately, then his memory started to go, and he could only teleport around the home itself. Or Starbucks.'

'Okay.'

'In England,' added Bill.

'Oh.'

'Ten minutes everyone,' a lady called from the canteen kitchen.

'Time called already!' cried Bill.

Trickster slammed the table. 'Damn! I was going to get another bowl of rice puddin' '

'It was nice to meet you, Son.' said Bill, as he stood up and shook Freddie's hand.

No buzz this time, instead Trickster slouched behind him, arms hung limp at his side and followed. His feet shuffled along the floor.

'Nice to meet you Mr Richard Richards,' Freddie said after the other two had left.

'It was my pleasure young man. Get working on that name, alright?'

Freddie laughed, 'yes, Sir.'

Freddie picked up the trays and took them into the kitchen to be washed when Valerie returned to see him.

'Did you have a nice time helping out?' she asked him.

'Yes, thank you,' smiled Freddie. 'I'm not sure if I helped anyone though.'

'Just seeing a friendly face means a lot. I will make sure to tell your uncle how great you have been.'

'Thank you,' Freddie said as Valerie showed him out.

Freddie got on his bike and smiled. Maybe the badge was worth the effort after all.

# **Train**

The boy full of innocence sat in the seat of the train. The world passed him by in reels of green and brown; local farm stock in the pastures, fields of lush green and dinky little houses he could hardly see. The world was so much bigger than he had ever dreamed.

Normally his world was contained in a small Cornish village where he was known by the whole community. Now he was anonymous, apart from his companion. Mum.

Two years he had waited for this opportunity and today it was finally here. Sam was going to London. Who knew what wonders awaited him? Sam knew it was huge, had Mum prepared him well enough? He knew he could not run. That was the hardest part. Running was a massive part of his life. His release. His therapy.

A man in a shirt and tie came down through the seats.

'Tickets,' he called. 'Tickets please!'

Mum passed the two train tickets to Sam. He felt a burst of excitement. His first ticket. What would happen? Sam passed the tickets to the man.

The man smiled. 'All the way to London, eh? You are going far.'

Sam laughed and bounced in his seat, the man laughed too and gave them back. 'Have a great trip.'

Sam held the two tickets tight in his hand.

'Would you like me to put them in my bag' Mum asked. Sam shook his head.

Mum laughed, 'Okay, you look after them.'

Sam gazed out the window. Boats floated on the water, and houses followed soon after. He recognised the bridge in the background, he was in Plymouth. There were two sets of rowers racing, buoys marked the posts. Sam counted the boats in the water, 47. A busy day, but the Tamar was a big river. There were 22 boats on the dock.

They were at Plymouth Station.

Sam crossed the station off a list mum gave him. It had the order of the stations between St Austell and London Paddington. It helped him come to grips with how long a journey it would be. 4 hours and 21 minutes was not an easy time to compute.

'We can go to the cafe to get a drink at Totnes,' Mum said. 'It's two stations away. It will be good to get up and walk about a bit.'

Mum was typing in her netbook, giving Sam some quiet time. She brought with her a pile of magazines and sticker books for him, but Sam couldn't concentrate on anything apart from the journey itself. Today was huge. Mum had explained there were going to be so many more risks and opportunities for danger. Especially with Sam's tendency to run off. Mum was the only person close enough to him to attempt this today. Although it was only one day in the capital, there were a lot of question marks about what could happen. He had asked for two years for this opportunity. He worked hard at school and was maturing. Sam was turning thirteen in two weeks, he was becoming a teenager.

Mum told him she passionately believed he needed opportunities like this. He would always need her, and his families help. After an honest and frank conversation with his teacher at Parents evening, Mum and Dad knew college education-wise was out. It was Life Skills-based schooling now. Mum explained her hope for GCSEs even if it took him until he was 25. Sam watched the fish in the classroom as they all talked. He could feel Mum was upset but unsure how to help. So, he fed the fish.

Sam's large hazel eyes studied their carriage. It wasn't full but different voices dominated the space. He leant against the window. His sandy hair flattened against the glass. He let out a laugh. Another station, Ivybridge.

Two more stations came and passed them by. They were at Totnes now, and as planned decided to attempt the café. They waited for people to settle and then stood up.

'Toilet too,' Mum said.

The toilet was a curved door with buttons to open, close and unlock. Mum stood outside to make sure no one came and disturbed him and gave Sam his privacy. Yells came from inside. Mum pressed the 'open' button. The door swished aside to reveal Sam panicking trying to open the door. Mum went inside and closed the door. Sam had seen her naked enough for her not to worry about anything he might see. Her privacy was a forgotten luxury.

They resumed the walk to the cafe. It was not easy. Legs, baby's feet, bags, people's elbows were hanging over armrests into the aisle. All were obstacles needing to be avoided which was a high demand for a boy with limited balance. Focus. Sam ran down the aisle, making Mum scream at him to slow down. The buffet carriage came into sight. A large group of men were in suit jackets with flowers at their lapels and a beer in their hand. Mum held Sam close.

Sam wanted to keep going. Mum stopped him and got him to choose a drink. Apple and Mango juice. A different kind from his usual. She got him his own brown paper bag which he accepted gratefully as he felt important and grown-up. Mum went in front this time to slow Sam down. They swerved their way through the group of men and thanked them as they stepped aside to let them pass.

Disaster. Halfway back to their seats, the train stopped at Newton Abbot. Bodies flooded the aisles making it impossible to pass without inconveniencing the other passengers. Sam pushed Mum ahead. Until now, it had gone smoothly. Sam had listened to instructions well and waited when he was told. Now it was a different story. Disruption.

Sam started to panic and yell. Strangers leant across invading his personal space. He could smell their deodorant; brash perfume flooded his nostrils. There were more items to take in. Silver suitcases, babes in arms. Sam and Mum kept moving, but then they were forced to stop.

A man was holding everyone up, as he tried to squeeze his bag on the shelf above his seat. Mum counted out loud to keep Sam calm, but the damage unfolded before her eyes. All her orders and preparation unravelled. The other passengers sensed the panic and tried to let them through. They smiled apologetically at Mum.

Sam and Mum made it back to their seats. A boy was in Sam's place. Mum asked him politely to move. The stranger could see the urgency in her eyes and apologised. Sam sunk down exhausted. He sipped the Apple and Mango juice, taking the change from his usual drink in his stride.

Sea flooded the view in the window. Saltwater curled and crashed against the stony shore. A lone windsurfer rode the waves and natural wind. People walked along the coast, huddled together, desperate for warmth. They smiled at the beautiful scenery. Red cliff edges came into the landscape and created a new world.

A flurry of tunnels. Sam looked out into the blackness, his reflection greeted him and within seconds the thundering red cliffs came back. Sea and stony beaches bordered the waves. Derelict ships rusted by the slow torture of time stood as a reminder of the past and misfortune.

Another tunnel. Ears began to pop. Random houses followed the red cliffs. More and more passengers erupted onto the train. Some boys started talking loudly, swearing, and laughing about bad haircuts and crap trainers. A family behind them argued over luxuries being requested despite a flood of money being poured into their trip so far.

Mum continued to work, and Sam watched the ever-changing scenery. A voice broke over the tannoy, different from the one from at the beginning of their journey. It told them about stations and cafe carts.

They pulled up at Taunton, a wasteland of dead grass and discarded road work equipment left for generations to discover. A flock of blackbirds flew in unison over the forgotten ground. No one was waiting at Taunton. No one wanted to get on or leave. A long line of bicycles in a row on the platform. One after another like dominos. Where did the owners of the bicycles go? No one was in sight. Sam saw a lake and dusty path from the window, fleeting images of new parents, students and workers in their daily lives, no idea they were being watched.

Flooded grass plains come into view, singular houses, lives existing as strangers passed them by. Little floods scattered and in contrast, neighbouring fields of crops appearing on the verge of extinction from drought. Shells of forgotten buildings, former homes of dreams that died with their fantasist. The buildings, a goal of generations lost, now just a frame, a skeleton to be commented on by walkers and ramblers oblivious to the importance of the shell presented before them.

But not all dreams die. The importance of a journey is evident for Sam and his mum. Having a challenging restrictive mind can bring great obstacles, ones not easy to overcome. Instead of accepting these barriers, brave people find ways to respect them, but also work around them. Sam found a way to embrace his best life and with his mother's guidance and belief in him, he needs nothing else to succeed. All dreams can be achieved, no matter what your circumstances, we just need to create the opportunity to live them.

# FAT GIRL DIARY

Day 1

08:30

Today is Monday and due to me noticing my dog, Noodle staring at my muffin top for a full eight minutes yesterday, I am on a diet. *Again*. No rubbish, just me and fruit. And veg. And coffee. Actually, fruit has sugar doesn't it? So, coffee and veg.

I've just looked in the fridge and I only have half a broccoli, although the stalk is still attached and that alone looks like a good meal. However, I do have mini gingerbread men. Ginger is good for your heart, isn't it? Yes! Coffee and gingerbread men. Diet sorted. Healthy living, healthy me. Oh, what a difference it will be.

I want to become an Ellie Parker. Ellie was a big girl, always very pretty- lovely smile and face and *really* nice. Everybody loves Ellie. Then she lost like, a whole person and now everywhere she goes everyone is like 'Oh my god, Ellie! You look AMAZING!' like capital letters AMAZING, which is the most amazing you can look. I want that to happen to me. Look out world- I'm becoming an Ellie!

11:00

I have finished my tub of mini-gingerbread men and drank 6 travel mugs of coffee. No chocolate or cake, even though I have an unopened pack of Cadbury mini rolls in the cupboard. How strong am I!?! This diet thing is a piece of piss! What is all the fuss about?

13:00

I have steamed my half of broccoli for lunch. I tried a bit of the stalk, but it tastes disgusting, so I left the rest. I waited for 1 pm even though I was frickin starving! Apparently, on the 5:2 you can add spices for no calories. So, I added nutmeg, ground ginger (looking after my heart ☐ ) and coriander. It tasted like crap! I could hardly eat it. Boo to broccoli, you green tree beast!

## 14:15

I went down to the village shop and got some feta cheese, dog food, lettuce, bread, and butter. Nice sandwich. Obviously, dog food won't go in the sandwich, but I thought feta is Mediterranean isn't it and those guys look healthy and tanned.

I would love to be tanned. I tend to go all red, peel like I'm the outside of a pomegranate and go white again. I tried fake stuff once, but I missed lots of bits I couldn't see. Ended up looking like a satsuma crossed with a dalmatian. Not exactly the best look. I don't have much luck with beauty. I shave, but only when we have a large supply of toilet paper or tissues. I cut easily; the last time so many strips of toilet paper were all over my legs I looked like a mummy in a horror film. I tried waxing but came out in red streaks. All over me! I was like a villain in a comic book movie ready to steal a nuclear weapon, or cappuccino maker from Costa.

The Mediterranean guys also seem to live forever, so that's good news for me. I also picked up some scotch eggs. Eggs are good for you, look at me filling up on protein. Maybe I should be a nutritionist.

## 14:40

After getting back from the shop I decided to watch some Netflix to pass the time. I put on *Friends,* I've seen each one loads of times but I chose a good one (The one with the Cop). It seemed to take forever to get to the *PIVOT!* Scene. I made more coffee because I got bored waiting for it.

## 15:00

I decide to go for a walk, that's a good exercise that doesn't involve jiggling about. I don't want to jiggle, once I start, I have no idea when I will stop and that is not healthy for my mind or self-esteem let alone the eyes of man.

Having a no jiggling rule, cancels out most exercise: running, jumping, aerobics, dance, pitch or court team sports like netball, basketball, football, tennis, badminton, and any others that involve other playmates having eyes to witness the waves of fat that will repulse them. Even if they did not hurl, I would be watching their gaze, thinking, "Are you looking at my muffin top?" And then I will try to sound less threatening by adding it wasn't a euphemism.

## 15:15

The walk is done, and I feel better for it. I have a shower after my healthy exercise, that's what people do right? I realise that I should have taken the dog. Noodle did look excited when I told him I was going for a walk. I will have to take him out later, my hair's wet. Unless I get the girls across the road do it. I have mini rolls to bribe them.

## 16:00

Thinking about the mini rolls made me eat a couple, after all, I have worked hard and deserve a treat. I decide to eat them differently just to give my diet some variety.

The first one, I was a bit eager and ate quite quickly. Just taking bites. I managed it in two. The second, I bit the chocolate off around the outside and unrolled it, licking out the cream. When I wondered which way was better, I decided I didn't care. Mini rolls are mini rolls and kind of wished I didn't faff about and just ate them normally.

## 16:25

A get a call from Mum and Dad, I tell them I am on a diet and my dad started to laugh. He asked me what the last thing was that I had eaten. I didn't want to say mini rolls less than half an hour ago, so I said broccoli. He asked how I cooked it and I told him with spices in the microwave. He said I should have boiled it. That sounds worse to me somehow.

He was impressed though and said it was good to cut out all the crap. Luckily, we were on the phone so he could not see my face. When Mum heard I had gone for a walk, she was impressed too.

## 17:00

My husband gets home and brings fish and chips. As we ate, he asked if I had walked Noodle. I told him I hadn't had time I had been so busy. He looked around the house and looked doubtful. Bit rude. I told him I picked up dog food and he said he had shopping in the car. We both went out and brought it all in and put it away. We also feed Noodle.

## 18:00

I go out and walk Noodle, my second walk today. I think along the way to the field. The shopping had lots of food that cannot go to waste. Maybe I should wait until we have eaten all that before starting a diet. If Noodle looks at my muffin top, then I will simply do what I should have done the first time. Lie down. Problem solved.

# THE SEA

Inviting, lustrous waves igniting the urge to come and play with me.

But I will warn you with my icy greeting,

I am dangerous, but in beautiful disguise

You will want to watch me in awe and serenity.

Foamy white swirls kiss the shore.

Seaweed fills my bed and slides under your toes.

I am an underground world for the living, voyages long-forgotten but sought.

I crash, I am tranquil, a mystery to explore.

Poisoned though protected and guarded by man.

My colours are rich and deep, so stunning they decorate your walls.

Do not underestimate my power, I am strong, fierce and unpredictable.

Yet I am so alluring I can be the sole reason to travel miles from around the world,

Some move an entire life to be by my side.

A wonder for the young, I am where memories are made.

Some cannot venture inside me through intense fear,

Yet wild swimmers discover a new way of living.

I can heal you, make you feel well.

I photograph well, inviting daydreams, but I also depict rage, devastation, or calm.

Exercise in me, bring your boards, your boats, your skis.

Explore me, find hidden treasures,

Read my history, my fables, my myths, my legends.

Write and sing shanties, become a songbird, worship me!

Listen to my stories of misfortunes and the secrets I hold within.

Hear my voice, the gentle murmur, the whisper I serenade.

But you must respect me.

I am the sea.

# Place of Mystery

As I walked along the lane with my brother and sisters, we saw a small overgrown footpath.

Jay the explorer, the brave one of us, raced ahead and we followed.

He stopped, 'Woah.'

Upon a bank was a gargantuan building. Walls crumbling away to nothing, disappearing before our eyes as if it were under a destruction spell waiting for a timelord to come and help save it.

'Look what I found!' he called.

'You never found it, Jay! It's not like it's the first time people have discovered a raggedy old building is it?'

'Shut up Martha,' Jay snapped. 'As far as I know, I am the first. We must investigate.'

'No!' my little sister yelped.

'It's okay Shelley, we just need to explore. Look at this place.'

It was the biggest building I had ever seen. And it looked like it had been left for billions of centuries. Maybe the Romans built it? Or the…someone else old.

I looked down at my sister, 'Shelley, Jay's right. We need to look around, how often do we find a place like this?' I held her hand.

The windows were tiny, so it must be ancient since before humans evolved from being goblins after we were apes. The gateways were narrow too.

'Let's start by going in here,' Jay said, as he ran and pointed to a gateway. Stone teeth hung down menacingly like a ferocious dog over the entrance.

My hand was pulled down. 'I don't like this. It's scary.'

'Don't worry Shelley, I'm with you,' I reassured her.

We edged inside but all that was there was a square of green grass, more walls and another passageway leading somewhere.

'Hey, look at this!' beckoned Jay rushing over to the corner. Martha ran over too. I took my time going over there with Shelley. She was hesitant but curious.

We caught up, 'what is it, Jay?'

'A bonfire,' said Martha, 'told you we weren't the first.'

Jay smiled, 'ah, but who made the bonfire?'

All I saw was a big stain of black and grey stuff on the floor. There was something else there too.

'It might be cavemen,' Jay continued, 'you know, so they could do their drawings, tell stories for the generations to come. Check the walls guys.'

Shelley and I stepped toward the walls and started searching. I only saw cold, lifeless stone. There was no sign of artwork anywhere.

'It's not cavemen Jay, there's a beer can in the ash,' said Martha.

'Oh,' said Jay. 'Hey! What's through here?' He darted through the passageway.

Martha followed and Shelley and I trailed after. This room was bigger. I looked up, where was the roof? There were massively tall walls, tiny doors, they could have split this into two storeys instead of wasting all the space on air. I guess this was before humans got smart and figured out how to build properly. In the middle was a gigantic circle like a massive firepit.

'Oh my God,' said Jay, 'this must be their torture chamber! They must throw traitors into this pit, don't go in there Shelley! You will never come out. A big monster is in there with gigantic teeth. He's bigger than our house! Right now he's sleeping, waiting to feed again and…'

'Really, Jay it's fine.' Whilst my brother was talking, Martha had climbed in and began walking around inside the giant ring. 'It's quite shallow really. I can feel the ground underneath.'

'I want a go,' I said as I came in, 'you too, Shelley?' She nodded.

'Well, if everyone is doing it,' Jay said with a shrug as he climbed inside.

We were all within the big stone circle and Martha was right it was shallow. Just like walking on the ground. If there was a monster he would have to break through. I am not daft, so I know we would probably hear him tapping or something first. If he were colossal, it would be pretty loud. I mentioned this to my brother and sisters.

Jay spread out his hands and whispered, 'let's be quiet and see if we can hear him.'

We all froze, even Martha and held our breath. We heard a snap, and Shelley screamed! Overhead, a bird flew from a tree and we all exhaled loudly.

'Let's keep going,' said Jay who forged ahead through another doorway.

This brought us outside which confused me. It looked like a labyrinth, a quest waiting to be explored. How could it be over already?

'It looks so big from the outside,' I said glumly.

'There must be another way,' replied Jay. He clambered down the grass bank to the front again and went running round to the other side. We shadowed his movements, and found steps leading up to a whole new part.

It was a wall of lots of squares with little hollow boxes and lined up in rows.

'What were these Jay?' Shelley asked

'Druids mixing pots, and witches' ovens. They used them to roast frogs for spells. We'll probably find some frogs legs if we look closely,' Jay explained peering in.

Shelley and I leant forward and nosed into the holes to see if we could see any trace of green or brown. It was just stone and black bits like they had been burnt.

'None in here,' called Shelley. 'We need to check them all. What if frogs are trapped and they have nowhere to go? And they are just waiting to be rescued?'

'Don't worry Shelley, we'll find them if they are,' I reassured. 'FFFrrrrooogggg!' I called into the holes.

'FFRRRRROOOOGGGGG!!!!!!!' Shelley screamed into hers.

'FFFFRRRRROOOOGGGGG!!!!!' Jay called.

Martha watched us but she did not shout into holes. 'I don't think there are any frogs inside the holes,' she said, 'maybe we should move on.'

'We can't!' screeched Shelley, 'not until we have checked them all!'

'Okay,' Martha said sulkily. She joined in too, 'Frog? Frog? Frog?' until we had checked them all. 'We have done it now. Can we leave, please?'

'Let's see what's beyond here!' said Jay as he hurried through another doorway.

We all ran after him and were greeted by another druids wall, we did not check for frogs. We were too excited by what lay before us. A tunnel. It was like a gateway into the 6$^{th}$ dimension or Narnia, we all hurried towards it. Boulders left by the ogres were sticking up from ground, which we had to climb over. It was fun going through it, not knowing what was at the end. It turned out to be just another room but with another opening leading outside again. I secretly wondered if we had found a treasury cleared out of its riches. We bounded through, down a slope and ended up back once again at the beginning.

There was one more archway we hadn't tried in the middle. That one was the most mysterious. The doorway was microscopic like it was made for animals or something.

'Wow! We must have found the ogre's entrance,' Jay said with awe.

Martha bent down to go through, 'I think you mean dwarfs. The ogres are like giants.'

'Oh. Okay,' said Jay, following after her.

I took Shelley's hand, 'Come on Shelley.' I led us both through.

Inside the doorway was like being inside a colossal pillar, it just went up higher and higher. We could hardly see the top.

'We found Rapunzel's tower! Wow!' Shelley announced excitedly.

I looked at Martha who was smiling at our sister, 'It very well could be Shelley. After all, Rapunzel's hair was crazy long so it would need an extra high tower for her to lower it.'

'I don't think it's Rapunzel, I bet it was here from a grim nasty king like Henry VIII and he kept prisoners in the tower to torture them.'

'Jay, I think it's Rapunzel's tower,' warned Martha.

'And I think it's the nasty king,' Jay said defiantly.

'RAPUNZEL!'

'KING!'

'Jay, I think Martha's right, I think it's Rapunzel,' I said.

'Yes, Jay. Its Rapunzel. We found Rapunzel's tower,' Shelley added sternly.

Jay gave in, 'okay, Shelley. We found Rapunzel's tower.'

Shelley smiled as she walked around, 'and up this wall is where the prince must climb to get to her. To make her his princess.'

'Sounds pretty lame to me.'

Martha gave him her best Mum look, 'Jay!'

But Shelley was still smiling, 'I think this place is magical. Thank you for finding it, Jay.'

Jay smiled back, 'my pleasure.'

'I think I would like to go home now though.'

'No problem Shelley. Let's go home,' Jay said as he took her hand.

She looked up at him and smiled, 'okay.'

We begin our journey home. Behind us, we hear the grisly witches cackle and the treacherous druids chant; glittery purple, black and green haze surrounds the tower. Rapunzel is trapped, the cold-hearted King has locked her up high, but a brave prince is on his way to save her. Savage ogres are climbing the walls trying to turn our world to rubble. Monsters surrounded by flames in pits of fire bellow deafening roars at the cavemen who imprisoned them there.     Freed frogs jump around our ankles relishing their escape from the druids cooking pots. We talk about how we could help them all and conquer our fortress once again. Our new sanctuary, the place we found together. Our realm of magic and curiosities. A creation of limitless outcomes and possibilities. Our place of wonder. Our place of mystery.

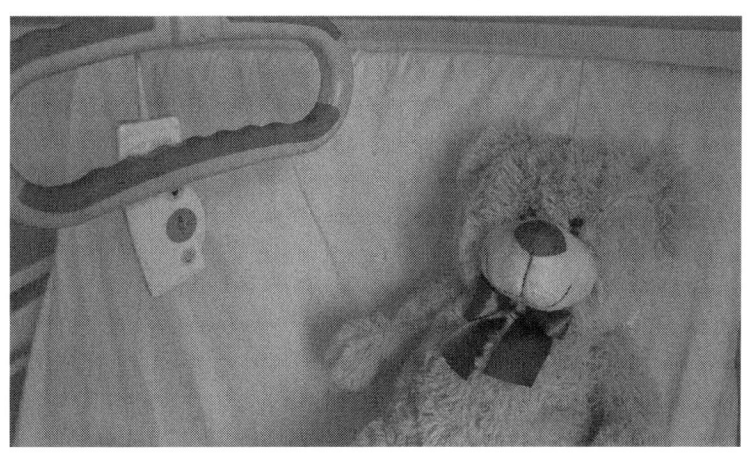

# HOSPITAL

Every bone, every muscle is tense as I wait. My mind is clouded, my head and body hurt. Sickness lurks in my stomach; I am just waiting for the moment when I can move. Families are chatting, and nurses laugh, while our bed is empty. I line up the presents, make it nice for when my little boy will appear.

An hour before, we were playing with cars as I gave my six-year-old son's details to the doctor. He took us into a small white room where I sat hugging my little boy on a single bed. My husband was waiting at the ward as only one of us was allowed to be there.

    I was told, 'hold him. In a few moments, he will go floppy.'

My son goes limp, as every bone seems to vanish inside his body. They move him to another bed beside me. I turn my head not wanting to see the blankness in my boy's eyes.

'Do you want to kiss him goodbye?' one of the nurses asks.

I cannot face it; I know from experience he will not feel it. He won't remember. The nurse leads me away. I hear the quiver in my voice, the tremble in my arm as she holds my hand. 'He'll be fine.'

I nod and push through the door to the stairs and back to the ward. Away from the lights, I let my tears flow.

Every minute since then has been a challenge, waiting for the word. The same questions asked over and over, name, date of birth, allergies. I don't ask my questions. Is it over? Can I see him? How much longer?

I wait. I know no news is good news. It is going well.

I tell myself, do not worry, if this is what it takes to make him well, then I must be strong. Whatever I need to do to be there for him, I will. I am his mother. He is my son, I am powerful. Resilient. I need to help him get through it.

My husband suggests a walk around the hospital grounds, but I cannot leave my son's empty bedside. I know it is fruitless as the operation will take thirty minutes, and it will take that again to come around from the anaesthetic, but I cannot move, I must be here. He brings me a cup of tea, but my thoughts are consumed with my son's face, I forget it and it goes cold.

The clock is loud and relentless yet sluggish. Half an hour passes over the time we were given. A solitary tear betrays my steel exterior as I imagine the worst.

A nurse comes around, she has seen us waiting.

'Have they not called you yet?' she asks cheerfully.

I shake my head. I cannot speak. Not yet.

'I'll give them a ring,' she says.

My heart beats faster, as I wait. Straining to hear what's being said. I curse the family beside me. Their son went after mine and is already back, awake and eating.

The clock continues its torment.

I take deep breaths.

'They're just waiting for him to wake up. We don't normally let parents down as it's not nice seeing them with machines. But, Mum, I said you're anxious. So, if you want to go down and sit with him it's okay.'

I love her. 'Thank you.' I get up then turn to my husband.

'It's okay. Go.' I have never loved him more.

I try not to run so the nurse can stay beside me and we go through the doors to the stairs. I was lucky she was with me as, in my haste, I had completely forgotten he wouldn't be in theatre. She took me to recovery where I found him. Small, sleeping, and perfect.

I can breathe again.

## Last Request

Gary couldn't wait to get home. After all his hard work, he had finally got the promotion he needed and worked for. He couldn't wait to tell his wife. He guessed Suzie would already have tea ready and waiting for him when he returned home as she was always eager to please him.

Putting his key in the door, he heard it click, Gary felt weightless. Like nothing could touch him. He came into the lounge where Suzie was sat on the edge of the sofa waiting for him. He rushed over, almost tripped over something but knelt in front of her and enveloped her hands in his.

'We did it Suz! Gerald told me today! I got the promotion. A third more than I am making now, and a bigger and better car. Gerald said the budget could be anything up to £200,000. I'll have to work and travel more of...'

Suzie was looking at the four hands on her lap. She gently pulled hers away as she stood up. 'That's great Gary, it is. I know that's what you wanted.'

Gary stayed on the ground as he tried looking into her eyes, but she kept her stare down. 'It's what we wanted,

Suz.' He started to stand up, but then paused as he saw what he almost tripped over. A suitcase. 'What's going on?'

'I'm going to stay at my mum's for a bit.'

'Why?'

'BECAUSE I CAN'T DO THIS ANYMORE!' She shouted. Her shoulders sunk. 'I'm sorry.'

'Do what? I get you everything you want.'

'Everything you want. I never asked for any of this.'

Gary sat on the sofa deflated. 'How can you leave me? We've been together since we were kids. '

'I know.'

'Well? Why then?'

'You are not my Gary.'

'Of course, I am!'

'No. You're not. You have been trying like crazy to impress Gerald. Just look at what you have become. You are obsessed with money. Quite honestly, Gary, I don't give a toss if we're broke and all this goes away. In fact, I would welcome it.'

Gary felt his body become warm and he started to twitch his fingers. 'Don't be so bloody silly. Of course, you would care.'

Suzie walked over to him, 'I knew you wouldn't understand. I have made you this.' She placed a cassette tape beside him. 'This will show you what I mean.'

She kissed him on the forehead, picked up her suitcase and opened the door. 'I love you, Gary,' she said as she walked out and closed the door quietly behind her.

Gary went upstairs to the bathroom, numb and eager to get out of his work clothes. He splashed cold water on his face, looked at himself in the mirror and went into the bedroom to change. He was angry. It was so ironic that he couldn't wait to get home. Suzie had ruined it, why did she do that?

On the bed was the old ghetto blaster, with a note.

*Thought I'd save you a trip to the loft.*

*Suzie x*

Gary saw the lead and plug were still attached, which he was thankful for as he wasn't sure if it would even work. He carried it downstairs, sat on the sofa and opened the cassette. Inside was a folded bit of paper.

On the inlay card behind it said *'Open paper after hearing the tape. Both sides!'*

He pressed play and turned the volume up. Music started to play.

Britney Spears's voice started to come over the speakers. 'Baby, Baby, how was I supposed to know...' It was from the night Gary asked her to be his girlfriend. They had always joked how they both hated the song, and it would now have to be in their wedding. Normally this would have made Gary smile, but he was too upset to care.

There was a pause and then 'Last Request' by Paulo Nutini began to play. This was the next song played that night when they sealed their relationship with a kiss. Their first kiss. Gary reminisced thinking about that moment and how long he had waited to feel her lips on his mouth. The kiss began soft and then they both leaned into it. There had many been kisses like that since but that remained the most perfect kiss he had ever had. He wished that he could feel it all over again. He looked at the space beside him on the sofa.

The memories kept coming through the power of music. Jack Johnson's 'Better Together', the album they always played when they had friends round eating cheese toasties, everyone sitting on the floor as they had no money for furniture.

'Heroes' by David Bowie was blasted over the loudspeakers when they crossed the finish line caked in mud after doing the 10k charity run; 'Can't Get you Outta my Head' by Kylie from when they were backpacking in Australia. They heard it playing in every bar they went.

Back then, Gary couldn't afford fancy gifts, so he borrowed an origami book from the library, wrote Suzie a love letter and shaped it into a swan. It turned into a little tradition every birthday and Christmas when he would gush about how much he loved her. When did he last do that? When did he stop? He couldn't remember.

Gradually Gary thought about the last time he even spent either of their birthdays not working. He couldn't. Life had got so hectic since… since when he wondered? It just kept escalating really. One day turned into a couple, the odd night became a weekly event, then he was working more of the week than not. Gary thought about how far he had taken all of this. His ambition controlled everything in their lives.

Gary tried to think of when he was genuinely happy. How long had Suzie known things had gone so far?

He listened to the rest of the tape, and he became more emotional with every song. Suzie was right, he had become a different person. He was no longer her Gary. He was the person they had always despised and pitied. A person who was only concerned with money. He would have to change and win her back.

Gary went to put the cassette back and glimpsed the bit of paper. He took it out and unfolded it. It was a sonogram; he was going to be a father.

A week later Suzie heard the postman and went to the front door to pick up the post. A small-padded envelope was addressed to her amongst the junk mail and bills for her mum. Inside was a cassette, and every song was about memories, changing and love. Beside the cassette was a piece of paper instructing her to read it after listening to all the songs.

When the tape stopped, Suzie unfolded the paper. Written inside was four words.

*I quit. Come home.*

Suzie smiled and went into the bedroom to pack her bags.

# **JEANNE**

On January 8th, 2013, Jeanne Manford took her last breath aged 92 surrounded by family. A year later a street was named after her, along with her husband and son.

In February 2013, the President of the United States, Barack Obama, talked about her to the nation and she was personally selected for the 2012 Presidential Citizens Medal, the second-highest civilian award in America. He had previously told her story in his televised speech at the Human Rights Campaign Annual Dinner in October 2009. This was during his first year of presidency, and he described her as *'the story of America. Ordinary citizens organising, agitating, and advocating for change. Of hope stronger than hate. Of love more powerful than any insult or injury.'* All Jeanne Manford did to deserve these honours and kind words was something that many women do instinctively. She stood up and protected her son.

Jeanne was no one special, you would hardly notice her on the street. She was a softly spoken Elementary (Primary) American schoolteacher from Queens, New York, neatly groomed hair, small in stature with a gentle demeanour. The middle child of five siblings, her parents were a salesman and housewife, and she started her career late due to being a full-time mother. She was blessed with three children but, in 1966, sadly her eldest son, Charles died.

Meanwhile, in the UK, homosexuality was legalised in 1967. In that same year, a book was published by Wainwright Churchill called *Homosexual Behaviour among Males*. Its revolutionary theory was that being gay was a fact of life, not a sin. But even though these were great first steps, there was still a lot of hostility towards the gay community. It was not enough the law had changed, people's minds and behaviours had to change too.

In 1966, a year before the law change in Britain, 420 men were arrested and convicted of gross indecency. And in 1974, that figure rose by 300% to over 1700 convictions. Many were sacked, thrown out of pubs and sexually assaulted.

People felt their entire emotional life was written up in the papers as utter filth and perversity. Hurrying to their GPs for help, the doctors conversed with their colleagues only to come back and say how their feelings were wrong and a sickness. Patients would then go on to have behavioural aversion therapy with electric shocks using photos of men and women in various stages of undress. They were told to use portable shock boxes for their fantasies and desires at home. The course of treatment would last anything from a couple of weeks to two years.

In America, in June 1969, the Stonewall riots began. After another raid at the Stonewall Inn, people actually began resisting arrest. There began a series of uprisings from the LGBTQ community, and new organisations formed such as the Gay Liberation Front and the Gay Activists Alliance.

People began to march for justice and for a world where they could have the freedom to be themselves.


On 15 April 1972, Jeanne Manford got a phone call. Her son, Morty, who was a strong activist and openly gay, had been fiercely beaten.

He was part of a small group of activists handing out leaflets at the Inner Circle Dinner at the Hilton Hotel, New York. Many officials had gathered for the annual event. The leaflets complained about the treatment of gays from the police. Michael Maye, head of the Fireman's Union got up and punched Morty. He then threatened to kick him down the escalator and the police did nothing. Morty ended up in the hospital. His sister, Suzanne, saw her brother's picture in the paper, '*I didn't even recognise him, He was so severely beaten.*'

As soon as she got the call, Jeanne dropped everything to be with him. As Morty lay there on the hospital bed, she was beside herself to act.

Full of outrage that anyone could hurt her child, Jeanne wrote to the New York Times, condemning the police for not doing their job and protecting him. She asked why the paper did not cover the story? The New York Times ignored her.

Determined, she instead wrote to the New York Post about the incidents and assaults and they published her letter. She stated publicly, '**I have a homosexual son and I love him.**' Her words spurred a massive response, highlighting and opening the discussion on violence against gays.

Morty called her after receiving numerous calls and congratulations that a mother would advertise having a gay son.

He remembered in 1989. '*We were on every talk show in New York City.*'

Jeanne added, '*We were the only people willing to go public. We felt it was a way to educate the public, making people understand.*'

Two months later, in June 1972, came the moment when Jeanne Manford became an icon. She took the Long Island train to Manhattan where it was pouring with rain, and then the subway. When she emerged, the sun was shining.

She stood beside her son in the Christopher Street Liberation Day March and proudly held a sign she insisted on making and carrying herself. It read, 'Parents of Gays: Unite in support of our children'.

Applause and tears surrounded her and Morty as they walked. By accepting and supporting her son, she signified all gay children should also be accepted.

It was the first time a mum or dad publicly supported their gay child. Jeanne showed the world gay and lesbian people had parents; they were somebody's children.

*'They screamed, they yelled, they ran over and kissed me.'* Jeanne recalled in an interview. *'They just couldn't believe a parent would do that. They were fearful of telling parents. Many had been rejected because the parents knew. I guess they just didn't feel that any parent could be supportive of a gay child.'*

*'It was unbelievable.'* Morty said. *'I'd been in the previous year's march and the outpouring of our own community was overwhelming. Nobody got the loud emotional cheers that she did.'*

A photo was taken, and it became famous as a pivotal moment in human and civil rights history. Letters from all over the world flooded in thanking her for standing up for them.

Nine months later, in March 1973, Jeanne and her husband, Jules, set up a parent's support group. Originally called POG (Parents of Gays), it gave parents a chance to get together. *'To talk to each other'* she explained. *'To know you're not the only one. Nobody was willing to let anyone else know about it. The immediate thing was to talk to parents and help them come to terms with the fact they have a gay child and there was nothing to be ashamed of, nothing was wrong with it, that he or she was no different than anybody else.'*

*'It was not so much what my mother said but that she said it.'* Morty continued. *'I remember her many times*

*saying there's nothing wrong with your son being gay or your daughter being lesbian. We've been taught by society that there's something wrong and society has been wrong. This is a civil rights issue. People had never heard this before.'*

The first meeting took place in a church basement in New York City, and Jeanne along with 20 other parents, LGTBQ people and allies attended. After that initial meeting, slowly calls came from across the country from people wanting to set up a group in their area. Today, there are over 400 chapters nationwide in America. It is the nation's first and largest family and ally organisation, with over 250,000 members and supporters crossing generations. People of the LGBTQ community who had always been hidden, ridiculed and tormented, now had a basis of support, education, and advocacy from families and allies.

When you think of the bravery Jeanne Manford had shown, the revolutionary step she took that meant so much to so many, it is easy to be amazed by the courage. Yet to her, it was nothing but a natural thing to do. Jeanne stated that she found a lot of parents felt the same as she did. They just didn't know.

Morty died from AIDS-related complications in 1992. He was just 41 years old, and his mother cared for him until he passed.

According to reports, Jeanne felt the march was a way of supporting her son. She wanted to protect him, let the world know that she stood by him, that he was hers. The photo of Jeanne and her son at the 1972 Liberation March was kept by her mantlepiece as one of her most defining moments, and she was proud that moment in history was recorded. That image also represented the fight for LGBTQ equality on the Civil Rights Float in President Obama's second inaugural parade; it was the first time that LGBTQ rights were included on that float.

In 1993, Jeanne was invited to become Grand Marshall at the first Gay Pride Parade in Queens, New York.

Although the law changed in Britain in the 1960s, it wasn't until 2003 that the Supreme Court decriminalised homosexuality in America. And it was only in 2010 that President Obama signed the Don't Ask, Don't Tell Repeal Act. This allowed gay, lesbian and bisexual people to serve openly in the United States Armed Forces.

I think one fact explains what kind of person Jeanne was. Amongst all the prejudice, hate and hardship it was felt by being gay at that time, whilst most kids were petrified of telling their parents who they were, to go through electric shock therapy to get 'cured'; Morty Manford asked his mother to march with him. He knew she would accept the opportunity and welcome it. Morty thought of his mother as *'a unique person.'*

Her daughter, Suzanne agrees. Speaking at a PFLAG meeting in San Francisco with her mum by her side, she said, *'My mother was never afraid. She loved Morty. Mum's biggest strength was it didn't matter to her. Gay or straight. She loved her child.'*

In an interview with Eric Marcus (Making Gay History), Jeanne stated, *'I always felt Morty was a very special person and I wasn't going to let anybody walk over anybody.'*

Jeanne Manford was brave, strong, devoted, powerful, and by her own admission, shy.

She was proof that no matter how ordinary you may seem; one revolutionary act can affect millions of lives all over the world. You can become a beacon of hope and give an outlet for others who are just as passionate as you are. Jeanne humanised and made people see beyond their initial assumptions to consider new perspectives. She fought for the LGBTQ community when no one else would and is now regarded as one of the fiercest fighters in the battle for acceptance and equality.

She was the mother of the modern ally movement, and she who changed history.

Photo: courtesy of PFLAG National

*"I love my son. And I want him to know how I feel. I want him to know I would do anything.*

*I am not a martyr.*

*Our children's lives are important,*

*I will do anything within my power to see that their future is good."*

JEANNE MANFORD

SPEAKING ON THE PAT COLLINS SHOW,

JULY 5, 1974

*One of the most painful things a woman goes through is losing her baby. One in eight pregnancies ends in miscarriage. No matter how many weeks you are along, when it happens you are a mother without her child. We need to talk more and be open about our experience. You never know how much it will help another mother in need.*

## PART 1:
## THE BABY

That fateful day

When her world fell apart,

When she rushed to hospital

And lost a piece of her heart.

A babeless mother soon to be

Up in heaven, her grandparents watched helplessly.

The clouds surrounded them. Pure, white as snow.

They held hands and shared tears at the scene down below.

'Help her. We beg you!

Stop all this pain!'

The grandparents pleaded with God to grant life once again.

'Or let us raise the baby until they can meet once more?

In many, many, years from now when her grieving is less raw.'

The mother screamed as the shock set in.

*How could this happen? When did she sin?*

It was too early to know if she was losing a daughter or son.

Before there was a breath to take, and its life had begun.

The mother felt empty.

Numb.

A strong sense of shame.

That it was something she'd done,

before she'd chosen a name.


Up high, God showed mercy. 'Okay, you may try.'

The Grandparents thanked the Lord as a shooting star flew through the sky.

# PART 2: THE GIRL IN THE CLOUDS

I gaze out the car window,
As the world passes me by.
My three children riotous in the back,
My husband driving by my side.
I look up and see her. A girl in the clouds.
I inwardly gasp as silence descends around.
I intuitively know she is my daughter,
And she is ten.
I never believed I could ever see her again.

I love her beyond being,
Her beautiful face.
She's been in my heart.
Never my arms.
She was never replaced.

Her hair draped around her shoulders.
My body is once more numb.
I would give anything to hold her.

To just be her mum.

Then I see them around her. My family that had died.
Different faces I recognised, as tears flowed from my eyes.
They are keeping her well.
 They plan to reassure.
Our lives mortally divided
After so much suffering to endure.

My daughter is growing up in Heaven, but now they must go.
I bless them. I whisper, 'I love you'.
But she already knows.

I thank them, for showing me the sign.
As I say goodbye to my daughter
For the very last time.

*The following blog post was written when the shops re-opened after the lockdown from the Coronavirus epidemic. It shows the madness of everything returning to normal (so-called).*

# **ISOLATION EASE? QUEUE HERE PLEASE!**

The whole of the UK has been waiting but hooray, the shops can now open. Sometimes shopping online out of boredom for everything from toothpaste to a llama just doesn't quite cut it.

For myself personally, it was a necessary trip. My daughter's feet grow quicker than Garfield eating a lasagne. She grew out of trainers on Friday, needed them on Monday. I also needed to return a present for my son, visit my local vinyl store and pick up some comics.

As you can see, I saved up lots of things that I could tackle at once (classic mum strategy). The return in the first shop started well, apart from the guy (his name was Alan) having his first day and told me no. I looked at Alan. It had been longer than 30 days. Behind him was a big sign that said returns were fine and being honoured within 30 days of the store reopening. I looked at the sign. I looked at Alan. I pointed to the sign and asked him to read it. Alan looked uncomfortable. Poor Alan.

He called the manager. The manager is ignoring him. He tries five times to get the manager downstairs. He then goes around the corner and finds him immediately. I suspect the manager thinks they are playing hide and seek.

The manager asks, 'what is it now, Alan?' Something tells me this has happened quite a lot today. I can't help but smirk (we have all been there Alan). He tells the manager he has a problem and points to me (literally). I am the problem. I explain, the manager looks at Alan and then reads the sign. Oh, dear. But alas, all sorted, and the manager runs and hides again waiting for Alan to call him down with the next customer.

So far, so good. Lockdown easing isn't so bad, but then I do the trainers. So, I go to the shop and there is only one-person queueing outside which is fine. So, I wait on my mark. For forty minutes. Yep. Several times I almost give up (I have no patience) but quickly the queue grew, and I was at the front, so I was a bit anxious to move and lose my spot.

We finally get in, I ring my daughter after choosing two overpriced pairs (you do not take a chance, that way if she hates them it's her fault, not mine!), this took 10 minutes and I go to queue.

The tills are divided into just two and there is no way you can choose closer to the end. Of course, I change to the shortest as soon as I get the chance and an hour later, I still have not moved. The man I was behind is now at the front of the other queue and there is no one behind me. I curse the people in my head behind him who are smiling at me. The NHS discount has confused my till and it has gone rogue. The queue for the other till is now so far back, the end could be in Narnia.

I cannot take it anymore. I dump the trainers and leave; I end up buying them in a clothing store instead. The rest of the time is fine, but unfortunately, I had already lost my sanity at the sports shop and had to overcompensate with a custard doughnut.

# The Two Trees

There stood two trees in a field.

One was big, breath-taking, and strong. Its branches scattered and thick, a climber's paradise. A rope swing hung from such a branch, inviting, and tempting young adventurers that came its way. The tree's leaves were so full and voluptuous, and their colours blazed so bright and healthy, it became the perfect view for the homes surrounding it.

Outdoor diners picnicked under its shade while children ran around full of laughter as they chased their friends and siblings around its powerful trunk. Initials etched from frozen moments of first kisses and embrace. Autumn brought new games, footsteps of imaginary dinosaurs and giants stomping wildly over the fallen leaves.

In the winter, cameras captured the trees glistening beauty from the frost and frozen raindrops, the images were saved as screensavers and made into cards to wish family and friends love over the season and new year.

Well-loved and captured, the tree was admired by all and described as majestic, magnificent, and remarkable.


The second tree was not thought about much at all. Its spindly trunk and spotted scattered leaves were small and ordinary. Its branches were too high to climb and it provided no shade for visitors. The tree was cropped out of photos and stood beside the tall, beautiful tree, ignored all year round.


150 years ago, a young teenage boy called Randal regularly sat against the spindly tree. Randal, like his resting place, was unnoticed by many. He was lonely and leant against the knobbly narrow trunk as he watched others play and make memories.

Randal's mum worked as a maid for a Countess. Sometimes, when she worked, Randal had to go with her. She was a struggling single mother and had no one else around so Randal would help her with her duties, which included cleaning out the Countess's bedroom.

One day, some jewellery was left out for an evening engagement that night. A striking diamond and sapphire tiara, bracelet and necklace were on loan to the much-admired Countess. Randal had never seen anything so fine-looking and stared as it sparkled in the light. He took them for his mother. She had so little and the Countess had so much.

Randal got home safe, but he was not prepared for how quickly news spread around the country, sparking outcry and shockwaves amongst every household. The scandal was everywhere, and frightening words like jail and prison were offered along with a reward to tempt and scare the public into action.

Randal panicked. His mum would be blamed, and lose her only source of income, her lifeline. She would be so upset and scared. Their names would never be forgotten or untarnished. So, he hid them. Buried them in his resting place, the one that no one noticed, underneath the spindly tree.

The jewels were never found. But only three years later, a terrible sickness took the lives of both Randal and his mother.

The mystery of the priceless jewels still stumped historians 150 years later as the spindly tree kept its secret well. For one and a half centuries, it concealed the most sought-after treasure the world had ever known and continues to do so to this very day.


Everything has beauty, but not everyone can see it.
**CONFUCIUS**

# TWO CATS

A scrawny ginger tabby cat, tiny in size
Looks and stares up the street in utter despise.

A big black cat strong and full-grown stares back.

Psyching each other out. Who will be the first to crack?

Minutes pass by and neither has moved
Neither cat relents, they have something to prove.
A car drives by, forcing Scrawny to flee
Big-Black watches. Filled with menacing glee.

Scrawny hides behind a branch covered in green

Big-Black lies in wait, not letting on Scrawny has been seen.

A battle of wits, full of patience and bluff,
Which one will win? Which one will get rough?

Big-Black peers around the corner and investigates where Scrawny has gone.
Big-Black hears him, pounces, but it's wrong!

Positioned on a stone, poking out from a wall.

It cannot see Scrawny behind the branch that did fall.

Big-Black strolls away, gently, not a hair out of place.

Scrawny bolts and Big-Black gives chase!

They run across the green bank at lightning speed!

Through all the gardens, around all the trees,

Screeching and hollering as they catch up and fight.

Then quiet as they disappear friskily into the night.

# **GARLIC PIZZA RECIPE**

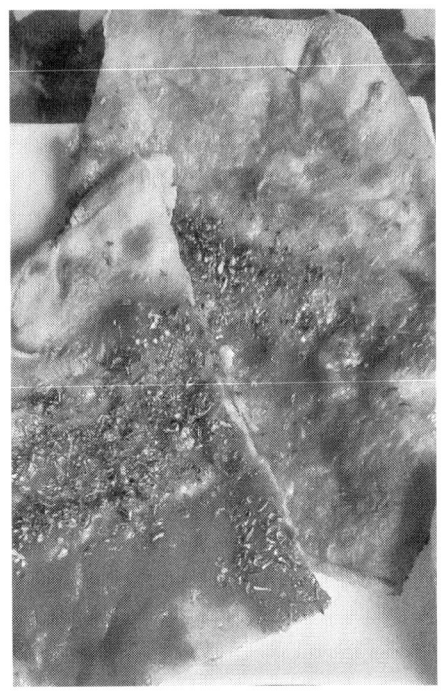

*Simple yet so delicious!*

*Serves 1 as it's a bit scrumptious, 2 if you like to share (but only if they deserve it.)*

You will need:

DOUGH: *4 cups of flour*

*Bit of salt*

*Sprinkle of sugar*

*2 cups of warm water*

*17g sachet of dried yeast*

*Extra flour for rolling dough*

*Napolina chopped tomatoes*

GARLIC BUTTER: *Fresh Garlic*

*Butter- room temp (or buttery spread, whichever is in the fridge)*

HERBS: *Fresh basil/ dried herbs or oregano and basil*

Oven temp: **MEGA** hot!

1. Put the cups of flour (any flour, we don't discriminate) in a bowl, add sugar (any sugar, not icing though, that would be stupid, we're not decorating) and salt (any salt. Table, Ummm...sea...) and mix.

2. In another bowl, add the yeast to the water and frisky whisk (whisk friskily, not feeling up whoever is close to you.)

3. Make a well (culinary speak for a hole in the middle) in the flour mix and pour in the yeasty water.

4. Mix well. (stand mixers are absolute diamonds for this. If you have one, use the hooky thing and rest your arms! You could even do a little mixxy dance!)

The dough is quite a wet one, sprinkle flour on the worktop and over the dough. Scrunch it up and move it about a bit till it's not so sticky. (Definitely brings new meaning to sticky fingers)

(Sid James would have had a field day with the above paragraph!)

5. When the dough is better, grab a wad (a good handful) and slam it on a chopping board or worktop covered in flour. Pick up a rolling pin (don't whack your husband with it, unless you are willing to wash it after) and roll it out as thin as you can without the dough breaking. Be brave, the thinner the better. Then put that bad boy on a baking tray laced with flour. If it breaks, squeeze it together. You are going to cover the top, so you have a bit of leeway.

6. Okay, mash up the garlic, if you love garlic put two fat cloves in. But if you just like it, you can just use one.
7. Get a good glob of butter (technical term) but about 75-100g and mix that with the mashed garlic together with a pinch of salt.

8. Spread the butter on the pizza dough thickly, add one ladle (just one) of the chopped tomatoes and spread it about. Add the herbs. Fresh basil is best but dried will do at a pinch.

9. Put it in the oven for 10-12 minutes until quite crispy. Then cut it up and eat it. Follow by sitting down and wondering how something so simple could be so tasty.

10. Repeat method the following night with remains of the dough, and maybe the night after that. Call friends and tell them how good a cook you are. Then impress them with it at your next movie night or get-together. Alternatively save it for celebrations, such as a day without rain or putting your socks on whilst standing up without falling over.

# MR. PERFECT & MS. IDEAL

### The Perfect Man would...
1. Be as handsome as Cary Grant
2. Be as cool as Samuel L Jackson
3. Have bravery like Sir Ranulph Fiennes
4. Don a body like Jason Momoa
5. Contain a calmness like the Dalai Lama
6. Survive like Bear Grylls
7. Have skills like Zinedine Zidane
8. Be as timeless as Laurel & Hardy
9. As ambitious as Alexander the Great`
10. Inspire like Barack Obama
11. Dance like Michael Jackson
12. Be as funny as Tommy Cooper
13. Create like Leonardo da Vinci
14. Have a brain like Socrates
15. Be as smooth as James Bond
16. Play guitar like Eric Clapton
17. Be as strong as Louis Cyr
18. Be as Fearless as Harry Houdini
19. Have imagination like Stan Lee
20. Draw like Michelangelo
21. Love like Giacomo Casanova

### The ideal Woman would...
1. Have a body like Marilyn Monroe
2. Be as brave as Rosa Parks
3. Have style like Katherine Hepburn
4. Care about the issues like Emmeline Pankhurst
5. Be as beautiful as Audrey Hepburn
6. Have ambition like Joan of Arc
7. Embrace ageing like Dame Judi Dench
8. Make an entrance like Rita Hayworth
9. Dance like Madonna

10. Be as funny as Fanny Brice
11. Be as breath taking as Cleopatra
12. Care for others like Florence Nightingale
13. Write like Jane Austen
14. Sing like Whitney Houston
15. Change history like Marie Curie
16. Bake like Mary Berry
17. As loving as Mary Bailey
18. Kickass like Boudicca
19. Rule the world like Queen Victoria
20. As mischievous as Harley Quinn
21. Be as iconic as Princess Leia Organa

*Even without all these elements or even one,*
*It's worth remembering when all is said and done,*
*You are perfect when you embrace your whole self*
*Being comfortable with who you are is worth all the wealth.*
*Aspire to be like these people and nothing more,*
*You are far more interesting than anything that has come before.*
*So, trust and believe in yourself, and become number twenty-two,*
*Because the ideal man or perfect woman you can be, will always be you.*


'You have to be unique and different, and shine in your own way.'

LADY GAGA

## **FAME-ILY PHOTOS**

Lily poured glue on the side of her robot's head and pressed both sides together. It immediately fell apart. She picked up the gloopy bit of cardboard and tried again, and this time pressed harder. It stayed put. Lily smiled. Then it slid down, along with her smile. 'MMMUUMMYYYY! IT WON'T STAY!'

'There's tape in the sideboard!' Mummy called in from the kitchen.

Lily walked over to the sideboard and pulled out both the drawers at once. She moved her hand around erratically, 'Mummy I can't see it!'

Another call came from the kitchen, 'keep looking! I'm just finishing the dishes!'

Lily pulled open the doors to the cupboard underneath. There were shelves of things but no tape. She pulled out what looked like books and the whole pile came crashing to the floor. Lily rummaged around further.

'Oh my God, Lily! Look at this mess!' said her mum as she walked into the room.

'I can't find it anywhere. I've looked everywhere, it's not here!'

The mum went to the top of the sideboard and picked up the tape, clearly on top. 'Here you go. I will put this back and you can clean this up.'

Lily gazed at her mother, 'will you help me?' She widened her eyes, 'please?'

The mum looked at her daughter's face and sighed, 'okay, but you must help too.'

'Okay,' Lily smiled, 'I promise.'

Lily started picking up the books and one by one placing them back on the shelves. Then she saw something peeking out underneath. Lily picked it up. 'Mummy, why is there a nudie lady in this picture?'

'What?' The mum stopped what she was doing and quickly saw what her daughter was staring at. 'Lily. Umm...'

'Who is she? Where are her clothes?'

'Okay,' she looked at the picture. 'This is a photograph of Great-Grandma Jean. She was a friend of Great-Grandad Arnold. We visited Great-Grandad Arnold, remember? Last Christmas? We went to his grave.'

'He was Granny Eleanor's daddy? Next to Granny Eleanor's grave?'

'Yes. That's right,' the mum held out her hand, 'maybe give that photo to Mummy now sweetheart.'

But Lily held on tight, 'Why doesn't she have any clothes on? Is she about to have a bath? Did she lose them? Where does she live? Does she not have shops?'

'You aren't going to let me have the photo back, are you?'

Lily shook her head.

'Okay. I guess you were going to find out anyway.' The mum started to pick up the fallen books and objects and started to put them away, 'help me clear up and I will tell you about Great-Grandma Jean.'

Lily smiled and put the photo on the table behind her.

'We will need this too,' the mum said, taking a photo album with a painting of a stream on the front from the fallen pile and placed it on the table beside the photo.

Lily and her mum put the stuff away and Lily grabbed the photo and book with the painted stream and carried them to the sofa.

'Don't you want to finish your robot?' the mum asked.

'Maybe later,' Lily replied.

'Okay. Well, hold on here. I'll be back in a minute.'

The mum walked into the kitchen and came back in with a cup of coffee. She moved the table closer to her beside the sofa.

'Okay,' the mum opened the cover and a small creak welcomed her. 'This album is very precious Lily. We must be careful with it,' she pointed to a photo. 'This is your Great-Grandma Jean.'

Lily leant in closer, 'wow.'

Inside were photos and news clippings. 'She's beautiful,' Lily said. 'Who is this?'

'That is Great-Grandma Jean's husband.'

'He looks like that picture of Grandpa.'

'A lot of men did back then. Shall I turn the page?' Lily nodded.

When the mum turned the page, there was a photo of a woman in a long sparkly dress, and one of her on a beach.

Lily smiled, 'she looks like a film star.'

'She was. She was a film star. A popular one.'

'Was she famous, Mummy?'

'Very.'

The mum turned the page again.

Lily pointed at the news clipping, 'hey! That's the man from Daddy's CDs.'

'Well spotted!' said Mum, 'That's Jack Abbott.'

'Was he a friend of Great-Grandma Jean?'

'Yes, they were good friends. They looked out for each other.'

'Like me and Molly?'

The mum looked at her daughter for a moment, 'yes, I suppose so.'

Lily's eyes darted over the pages in the book, 'are there more people from Daddy's CD's?'

'I don't think so. It's been a while since I looked at these. Shall I turn the page?'

Lily nodded, 'are there any pictures of Great-Grandma Jean with Great Grandad Arnold?'

'No.'

'Why?'

The mum looked at Lily and wondered whether to go on.

'Okay,' she began, 'your Great-Grandma Jean was married when she met Great-Grandad Arnold and they fell in love. He came round to clean their cars to earn money. Great-Grandma Jean told him to come back every day after that to clean their pool. Your Great-Grandad was only 16 at the time and had no idea how to do it, but she kept asking him to come back. Great-Grandma Jean was gorgeous but also very lonely. She liked your Great-Grandad very much. So much they had a baby together.'

Lily looked at her mum, 'they did? Was that Granny Eleanor?'

The mum nodded. 'But there were a lot of people who did not like them being together. Your Great-Grandad was incredibly young, and Great-Grandma Jean had a whole life controlled by lots of important people.'

'Were they bad people? What did they do?'

'Well,' answered Mum, 'they needed to stop a scandal and they threatened to take the baby away from them forever.'

Lily gasped, 'oh no!'

'I know. Can you imagine if someone said we could not be together and wanted to take you away?' Mum said.

Lily grabbed her mum by her top, 'don't let them, Mummy!'

The mum put an arm around her daughter. 'Don't worry, no one's going to take you away. But you can see how frightening it is. And these people had a lot of power.'

'So, what did they do?'

'They planned to run away and hide.'

Lily gasped again, 'did they do it?'

'Not all of them,' The mum said, 'just Great-Grandad Arnold and Mum.'

Lily looked confused, 'you?'

Mum shook her head, 'no, sorry. I meant my mum, Granny Eleanor.'

'So,' said Lily, 'what happened to Great-Grandma Jean? Did she come later?'

The mum stroked the album page with her finger, 'she tried, but she was followed and made to stay in her house. She divorced her husband, but they still wouldn't let her see her baby. It's tragic really. You see, in those days it would have been a huge scandal. Great-Grandma Jean was a lot older than Great-Grandad Arnold; it was only just legal. If they had gone public, all her popularity would be gone.'

'And that would make Great-Grandma Jean sad?'

The mum smiled, 'Great-Grandma Jean didn't care, she would have lived in a shed if it meant they could be together, but she made a lot of people a lot of money. They gave her no choice.'

'So, did she never see Granny Eleanor again?'

'Yes. She managed to sneak in a few visits before she died.'

Lily looked worried. 'She died?'

'Yes, a few years later but Granny Eleanor always remembered her.'

'Was Great-Grandad Arnold sad?'

'Very. But he was a great dad and although it was hard work, he raised Granny Eleanor all by himself. Then in time, he met Nanny Leona and he fell in love again.'

'Did Nanny Leona mind this picture?' Lily held out the nude photo.

The mum laughed, 'I don't know.'

'How did Great-Grandad have it?'

'He was in her house and a book was being made about her featuring lots of photos. She told your Great-Grandad to choose some if he wanted. She suggested he should have the nude photo.'

Lily's eyes widened, 'did she not mind?'

'No, she did a calendar that made her famous. Most people had seen her naked.'

Lily gave a nod, 'can we look at the pictures again?'

The mum smiled, 'okay.'

There was a big photo of a woman with lots of cameras pointed at her.

'Why are they all taking her picture?' asked Lily.

The mum smiled, 'she was filming that day and lots of people thought she looked really pretty. That turned out to be the most famous picture of all time of Great-Grandma Jean. Lots of people have that on their walls even now.'

'She must have been lucky and felt special to be loved by so many people. And to end up on people's walls.' said Lily

The mum kissed her daughter on the head, 'I guess she was.'

'And beautiful.'
'She was. Extremely beautiful. Just like you.'

Lily smiled and looked at her mum, 'like you too, mummy.'

The mum smiled.

Next, there was a big poster of a film.

'Was Great-Grandma Jean in this film?'

'Yes.'

Lily leaned closer to the page, 'I can't see her.'

'She goes by her stage name. That's a name you use when you perform. Musicians and actors use them.'

'What was her stage name?'

Mum closed the photo album and put it down. 'I'll tell you what, let's have some ice cream sundaes and I'll tell you after.'

'Okay,' Lily smiled, 'did Great-Great-Grandma Jean like ice cream sundae's?'

'Every day after acting class, they were her favourite! She taught my mum how to make the best ones, and now I will teach you. It's our family secret.'

I have tried with all my might,
To try and come to terms with that fateful night.

When my baby brother left me, no warning. So quick.
I am heartbroken, engulfed with dejection and sick

For Don **FOREVER 36** x

I always feel a bit empty,

my heart is not full
I try to be normal with housework and school.

My world is faded, a little bit grey,
I keep reliving the moment

you were stolen away.

I was meant to protect you.

Keep you safe and well.
I have so much to say to you, so much still to tell.

My children will love and know you,

I promise you this.

You will forever be in our lives,

although your love we do miss.

Along with your strength, hugs, smiles,

the way you held my hand,

I know there's no answer, no way for me to understand.

My handsome brother.

My children's best friend.

I'm not okay.

I cannot pretend.

I see you in rainbows and the brightest star,
That does give me comfort.

It makes you feel not so far

Today is your birthday,

I send wishes to the clouds above.
I hope up in heaven you can feel our love.

*The idea for this piece was to show the stage in relationships that aren't talked about enough, but most of us are in. Not the new love, or the scandal breakup but the part of a relationship where you have been together for years and are comfortable with each other. You live day to day relying on the other person to be there, you have grown into a team that instinctively knows habits and the little ways of the other person. The normality of happily ever after.*

## **THINGS I MIGHT NOT SAY**

***I know I may not express it but...*** I am thankful for who you are. You are the one I always thought about when I imagined my perfect life. I was never just myself before you. I was always worried no one would accept me as I am deep inside.

***I know I may not tell you but...*** I never imagined having a partner who, even when they didn't understand my fears, respected me enough to sense their value and how they affected my world within.

***I know we don't declare it but...*** I never believed my children would have two parents united in thought and plans. Although no future is set, minor goals we work together to complete.

***I know we don't talk about it but...*** I know neither of us is perfect, we both have flaws that could grow if we let them. Knowing these shows our intimacy and tolerating them shows our commitment towards each other.

***I know I may not confide in you about it but...*** My biggest fear is you finding someone younger and new. Although I would survive, my investment of time, love and trust built over the years could never be replicated. I would never have the opportunity to begin again where a lifetime shared was the hope.

***I know I may not always show it but...*** I plan to grow old with you. Believe in me as I believe in you. Believe in us.

***I know I may not say it but...*** I love you. Even if we destroyed each other inside and demolished the life and love we both share, I will always love you. You will always be my husband, no one will ever take your place. You are and will always be, the love of my life until I take my last breath.

# THE DANGER OF BEING THE

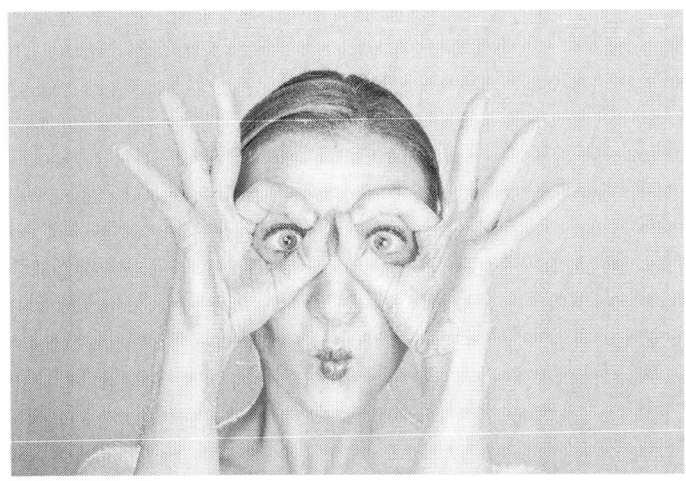

# FUNNY ONE

Everyone tries to come out of their school days unscathed but there is one type of person that seems to struggle to leave that teenager behind. I am one of those people. I was the podgy funny one. I wasn't skinny or athletic who then got fat. I wasn't the drop-dead gorgeous teen who was massively popular but now works behind the counter in a fast-food restaurant, I wasn't the overlooked average build who achieved great things and became a happy success. No, I was rubbish at sports, I was tall so could get cigarettes from the petrol station (in school uniform, which apparently was made invisible by my height). But I could come out with a good quip now and again, and I would literally do anything anyone asked me to. My friends were the ones with cute boyfriends a couple of years up or from the rival school. I was mostly ignored apart from our little group but strangely everyone in my year knew me on a friendly basis.

In college, I became the funny quirky one with a huge crush on dreamboat Robbie, who wore his trousers under his boxers and looked like Rob Thomas out of *Matchbox Twenty*. He also had his own entourage which made him cool. Not like me, the funny quirky girl who wore check pyjama bottoms in the halls and played a card game called 'Raps' in the common room (If you lost, a pack of cards was scraped against your knuckles in a clenched fist). Bloody knuckles from a funny girl wearing sleepwear. Not exactly material to get the boys lining up!

Along came adulthood, and I was popular with boys because I could down a pint, play pool, my chest was big, and I liked football. As my friends would win them over with alluring glances, I would charm them with my likeable personality. Both worked, I just needed a bit more time to perform my seductive trick than they did for theirs.

The men that came my way normally had a few beers in them to make things easier. Whenever I would be paid a compliment, I would look around to see who they were talking about. I usually presumed they were just trying to get me into bed.

If a guy comes along and is genuinely bowled over by you, it takes a while to believe it. And once you do, you marry him. My husband is the only one I genuinely believe when he compliments me or calls me pretty. He doesn't have to try to get me to do anything, he has me. Just like I have him to pay for petrol. And pizza.

When I became a mother, I embraced pregnancy so much I would eat whatever 'baby' wanted. The truth was baby knew nothing about beanburgers or Mars bars, it was me. I wanted to eat a lot. Apart from cravings I could not control, it was a blessed opportunity to eat like a pig for 9 months. No one could judge. After all, I was eating for two. But then you become one again and your belly for two stays, you begin to wonder 8 months later, how long you can say *it's because you just had a baby*. After their 1st birthday, that excuse is a bit thin.

So, funny and fat now. Cliché city.

>Worse still? Loud.

>Funny, fat, and loud. Good grief.

Three kids in and I have finally found the secret of most successful way to lose weight: Eat better, eat less, move your ass off the sofa and do some bloody exercise. Who knew?

>If it involved eating less chocolate or drinking less wine, I always wondered if it was worth the risk. If I found it hadn't worked, I would have deprived myself for nothing. And both chocolate and wine are far too scrumptious for that.

>Turns out it was worth it as it actually works, or it did for me. Afterwards, you go down to a size that isn't a plus, and are considered "normal", and inevitably people notice. Especially when you look like something the previous you could have enjoyed as a snack.

>But when they say:

>'*You've lost loads of weight*'; my reaction is *how heavy was I before*?

>'*Your hair looks nice today*', I think *does it normally look like I've been dragged through a bush?*

>'*You're looking well*', immediately embraces the thought that I usually resemble a turd.

>'*Wow! Look at you!*' Is practically screaming *Oh my God, you look almost human*!


>Some of these may scream low self-esteem, but the credibility of these compliments is usually reserved for my friends. I'm normally the girl less under a spotlight and more at the back handing out popcorn providing a commentary. I

dress quirky and I am still loud because I am comfortable with who I am. The girl who makes you laugh, the one with the likeable personality,

If you call me pretty, I look round and presume you are talking to the flowers in the garden behind me. I will never react properly. Instead, I turn into a bumbling Hugh Grant and make a prat of myself. I'm afraid it will likely always happen, that is the danger of being the funny one.

Once you have been fat, you only see fat. Once you've been overlooked, people always seem to be talking to someone else. And once you are 'the funny one' that is your persona. Not sexy, not gorgeous, but funny. And I'm okay with that. After all, I'm the one who gets to make people smile, which is kind of cool, and I embrace it.

# **THE PERFECT WIFE**

To the outside world, Vanessa Barrington was perfect. She was happily married to a wonderful man with a good job that paid the mortgage. A mother to two beautiful children, with blonde hair and blue eyes. They were always quiet, clean, and well behaved. Vanessa herself had long blonde hair tied back in a ponytail, a slim figure and excellent taste in clothes. Although she didn't work, she volunteered for every group in the community from the PTA to the village hall and the playing field committee. Vanessa was charming, knew everybody and had white teeth and an easy smile. The other mums that knew her, believed she was confident, accomplished, caring, beautiful and a lovely person to know. She had her life together.

Inside, it was a different story. There was a lot Vanessa Barrington never told anyone. She never told anyone that although she loved her life, she felt trapped. She longed to feel valued and needed. When she was young Vanessa wanted to be an artist, but she never believed in herself. She enjoyed projects that came with volunteer work as it gave her a chance to be creative. Something she was too cowardly to pursue in case people laughed because she wasn't good enough.

She never told anyone that although she loved her husband, they had been together a long time and had little passion left. They had grown to middle age together and although she had tried to embrace it, she was desperate to feel young and still attractive. When she had their first baby, Vanessa put on a huge amount of weight, she became depressed and never wanted to see anyone or do anything. When she looked in the mirror, she saw only ugliness and was now petrified of feeling so low again. She wished she could have the relationship she had when they first got together, and her husband would constantly touch her body. Any excuse whenever he passed her. Sex had become routine and was no longer exciting, new, or engaging. She wanted to explore new ways to enjoy each other, but her husband was reluctant and resistant to change. As long as they loved one another, they were fine.

Vanessa never told anyone that, as much as she loved her children, they drained her energy and attention. They constantly needed her, and never left her alone. Suffocating under the strain, all she felt for them was love but resentment kept creeping in. She remembered when she was young, always out with her friends, her family only saw her at dinnertimes. Her children stayed inside staring at the screen. She knew they shouldn't watch for too long, but it made things easier and it was what she needed to get through the day. Sometimes they went out for walks and they would enjoy it, but she had to negotiate or blackmail them to take part.

She never told anyone how lonely she was. Her friends all had families of their own, coping day to day just like her. Not wanting to be a burden or impose on acquaintances, she joined community volunteer groups to give the illusion of friends; and meetings at the pub turned into nights out she looked forward to and dressed up for.

Her own family were not around. She would watch films and see the bond between family members or in a new romance and feel jealous and wish it were her. She thought about old boyfriends and times when she was surrounded by friends when she was young. Deep down she knew, it was because of how uncomplicated her life was back then. Now she was so much older, youth and carefree was what she missed.

To Vanessa, every other mum she met seemed happy. She envied the ones that worked and set up their own little side business. They had something just for them. Everyone else seemed to be surrounded by friends and have men crazy about them. They were secure and fixed in their lives. Busy with pals, meeting for lunch or sharing perfect days on social media.

From the outside, Vanessa Barrington was perfect, with the perfect family and perfect life. But to Vanessa, it was everyone else who had perfection and all she was left with was coping, living as best she could and desperation not to feel so alone.

The only thing Vanessa longed for more than anything, was someone she could confide in. Let down her guard completely and have them say, 'actually you are doing okay.'

She was failing, more and more every day and it was only a matter of time before the world realised how much. And then the judgement would come.

*(I can't breathe, I can't breathe, I can't breathe, I can't breathe)*

Gasping for air

Extinction via protection

Overpowering force

Racial disgust full of ignorance

G*od, please take care of my mama*

Eight minutes, 46 seconds of pressurised hell.

*(I can't breathe, I can't breathe, I can't breathe, I can't breathe)*

Fighting only for air

Leaning evolves into a weapon of death

Only cold metal holds my hand for comfort.

Yelling, begging one last time for mercy; Let me move.

*(I can't breathe, I can't breathe, I can't …)*

Darkness.

## Black Lives Matter. Humanity Matters.

The guidelines for the brief to this story was to make it dialogue only. It was interesting and fun to write, and I had to think carefully about how to get a plot across using only speech. I hope you enjoy it, and if you enjoy a creative challenge, maybe have a go at one yourself.

# **PRIZED SECRETS**

'Are you sure you want to do this last segment, Sir? We can still change it. We got the other questions ready to go.'

'Of course, I do! It's going to be epic. Just imagine the hits on YouTube alone. Just remember to get some really good close-ups when the magic happens.'

'Okay. Boss says we're a go everyone. And we're live in 3…2…1…'

'Hello, and welcome back to the final part of Kids Spill All. Andrew and Felicity from Cheshire have beaten off the competition to play for our Star Prize: an all-expenses 5* trip to your dream location, Disneyworld Florida! Not only will you travel First Class, but you will stay in a Deluxe Resort Hotel with $1500 spending money. Tell me, Andrew and Felicity, what would this prize mean to you?'

'Well, everyone at the kids' school has been to Disneyworld and we simply can't afford it. It's way too expensive for the five of us, and Andrew's recently had to take a pay cut from work…'

'Felicity! I thought we weren't going to mention anything personal.'

'Oh, come on Andrew. No one we know watches this show, no one's going to find out. We …'

'Okay, let me just stop you there, Felicity, as its time to play our final game. Only two more secrets left to reveal. And what do secrets mean everyone? Secrets mean…'

**'PRIZES!'**

'That's right. Now, if you guess our first secret, you win a great prize. But if you guess our second secret, you win that fantastic all expenses paid trip to Disneyworld, so your kids won't get bullied.'

'We never said they got bullied.'

'Not something you like to talk about. I understand. Now, we asked your three children Annabelle, Thomas, and Verity, what is Mum and Dad's biggest secret? What did they say? Let's start with Mum.'

'Oh no!'

'Don't worry Felicity, if you go first, it gets it out of the way. And if you guess correctly, you win this wonderful set of gardening tools courtesy of our good friends at grasscutts.com. Now, Felicity, what do you think Annabelle, Thomas and Verity said was your biggest secret?'

'Gosh! I don't know!'

'It's okay, we have options! Let's look at them. You have, a. Mummy steals money from daddy when he isn't looking, b. Mummy hides our chocolate from Easter and eats it secretly, c. Mummy has lots of parcels that she hides from Daddy or d. something else?

'Oh my God! How horrifying!'

'Do you steal money from me?'

'Of course not! Let's say the chocolate one.'

'Okay. Chocolate.'

'Okay. You chose b. Mummy hides our chocolate from Easter and eats it secretly. Let's see what Annabelle, Thomas and Verity had to say. Run the VT.'

'Mummy has lots of visits from different men. They bring lots of parcels for her every day, but Daddy tells her off for buying things from shops, so she hides them in her wardrobe.'

'Mummy likes to take our chocolate from Easter and gobbles it all up when she thinks no one is looking. '

'She does that at Christmas too!'

'She ate my chocolate reindeer once!'

'Mummy also goes through Daddy's dirty clothes looking for money. Then she says, "I'll be back in a minute", and "Annabelle's in charge".'

'Yes! Mummy says I am in charge because I am the oldest. And then she comes back with her special drink, the one we are not allowed to touch.'

'And she drinks it before Daddy gets home.'

'And then hides the bottle in the cereal cupboard.'

'Oh, what precious angels they are! I'm afraid the correct answer to that one was d. Something else. All three were right! A little bit tricky that one! I bet you'll have some words for those scamps when you get home, Won't you Felicity?'

'Umm...'

'Lost for words, eh? Well, remember, Kids Spill All. I'm afraid you don't win the garden equipment, but you still have a chance to go on that dream family holiday to Disneyworld. Let's try and get this next one right and get you all on that plane.'

'Okay, we're ready.'

'Fantastic Andrew. This next one is all about you. What did your kids say when we asked them what Daddy's biggest secret was?'

'That I pick my nose?'

'Let's see if it comes up, shall we? Here we go, look at that! a. Daddy picks his nose and rubs it into the furniture. You saw that coming didn't you Andrew!'

'I had a feeling.'

'Fantastic stuff. Well, you can go with that or you can choose one of your other options. We have b. Daddy locks himself in the bathroom for ages and won't let anyone in. c. Daddy picks food up off the floor and eats it, or d. Something else?'

'Every man does a, b and c! How come he gets off so easy!'

'I agree with you, Felicity, it is a puzzle. What did your children say was Daddy's little secret?'

'I think d. something else.'

'Andrew? What do you think? Do you agree with Felicity?'

'Yes. d.'

'Okay, you're going with d. Let's see what Annabelle, Thomas and Verity had to say. Let's run the VT.'

'Once, it was Mummy's birthday and Daddy was late.'

'Yes! We rushed out with some cake, and Daddy was doing his special face tickles with a lady with red hair.'

'He was tickling her under her coat too!'

214

'We saw her underwear!'

'She had underwear like Mummy but nicer.'

'It was red!'

'I like Mummy's underwear more.'

'Daddy said a lot of naughty words.'

'Daddy paid us each a whole five pounds to keep quiet!'

'He said we couldn't tell anybody because Mummy would be angry.'

'We tried to give the lady some birthday cake, but Daddy told us off.'

'Then he took us to McDonald's the next day and we swore we would not tell.'

'We had Happy Meals!'

'He made us promise.'

'We promised we wouldn't tell.'

'And we didn't tell Mummy!'

'No, we didn't!'

'We kept our promise!'

'We made Daddy happy!'


'Oh, dear! I don't think they did make Daddy happy did they, Andrew?'

'Umm...'

'WHAT THE HELL WAS THAT!?! ON MY BIRTHDAY? WHAT THE HELL ANDREW!?!'

'I am so sorry, Darling.'

'DARLING!?! DON'T CALL ME DARLING! YOU CHEATING SON OF A BITCH!'

'Felicity, I can see you are a bit excited but please remember we are live...'

'I COULDN'T GIVE A SHIT YOU ARROGANT LITTLE PRICK!'

**'Ooohhh!'**

'Oh my. Felicity please calm down and watch the language, you're getting the audience excited. The great news is you...'

'ON MY BIRTHDAY! Who was it? Whose face were you getting off with? Was it that slut, Anna?'

'Please don't call Anna that.'

'So, it was her! I thought you weren't going to see her, again? That we were going to have a fresh start?'

'I wasn't. We were. I didn't plan it. It just kind of happened.'

'Bloody hell! The children! The children saw, and you bribed them! What the hell is wrong with you?'

'I don't know. I panicked. It was a mistake. Big mistake. Can we talk about this later? I am so sorry Darling.'

'And you took them to McDonald's! YOU KNOW I HATE MCDONALD'S!'

'I know, I know.'


'Well, like I was saying, great news! You got the answer right which means ...'

'Oh God, did you bastards know? Did you plan this whole thing? You ask the kids a whole pile of questions and this is the one you choose?'

'No one can predict what secrets the kids will spill. But guess what? You got the answer right which means you've won…'

'DID YOU KNOW!?!'

'Which means you won that all-expenses-paid trip of a lifetime…'

'YOU DID! YOU SON OF A BITCH YOU SET US UP!'

'Felicity, stay behind your podium… Felicity, go back…'

'**OOOHHHH!**'

'YOU BITCH!'

'Felicity, what the hell did you do? Oh my god, where did they come from?'

'Please step aside sir. Michael Ashford, do you wish to press charges?'

'Yef. The bifth broke my nodse!'

'Very well. Felicity Bryan, I am arresting you on suspicion of assaulting Michael Ashford. You don't have to say anything. But it may harm your defence if you do not mention when questioned something you may rely on later in court. Anything you do say may be given in evidence.'

'Don't worry darling, I'll get the lawyer sorted. Don't worry about a thing, I'll meet you at the station!'

'Please Andrew, don't let the kids find out! Get to them right now!'

'Will do!'

'Wrap it up, Michael.'

'Ples join mush agin fmor Kids Spfill All. Goodbye.'

'And we are out in 3...2....1....'

'Bloody hell! Fiery one that Felicity! Good job we had the police waiting just in case.'

'Is Michael alright?'

'First aiders are seeing to him, he might have to go A&E, but he should be fine for tomorrow's show.'

'If there is a show tomorrow. Sorry Sir, that was a disaster!'

'What are you talking about? Better than I could have dreamed! TV Gold. The ratings are going to be through the roof! We just made history. Let's go to lunch! Don't worry, Mike will be okay, and we'll get him to drop the charges. That's going to be one hell of a holiday! Well done guys. Good job everyone.'

'You heard him, that's lunch. It's a wrap everybody!'

# RAINBOW

I see the colours across the sky,
Darkness dominated before this time.
Grey, dense, and crying tears of rain,
The world can breathe new life again.

Nature's way of saying, *'Don't be sad.*
*No matter what appearance may say, it's not all bad.*
*Darkness comes, but the light will follow*
*There will always be a new tomorrow.*
*Don't lose hope instead see beauty once again.'*
Nature's children satisfied, fed from the rain.

For those who lost someone dear,

A celestial arch shows they are near.

Always watching, keeping you safe and well.

The light has begun, a new chance begins now.

# A Bar Tale

'Come by on Friday night.
We'll go down the Queen's Head,
It'll be a laugh, we'll have a few drinks'
My sister and her husband said.
The bar was packed, the pub was full
What is causing all this fuss?
But then I hear the ivories,
Of a piano playing behind us.
I turn around and try and look
To watch the musician play,
My sister's husband gets the round
After moving the punters away.
I clear a path for us to move
To the corner of the pub,
A lady is on a piano stool
And I fall instantly in love.
The girl has brown curls,
Cascading around her shoulders.
I stand up and move close,

I want to kiss and hold her.

I watch her singing with that lovely mouth,

Her voice not quite as good,

But the woman played a happy tune

With all the gusto she could.

Her eyes are chocolate brown,

Her laugh infectious and loud,

I am desperate for her to notice me,

But there are fellas all around.

My sister comes up behind,

She pulls me back across the room.

I will have to wait for her break

But I will return soon.

My sister and her husband chat,

I'm not listening to anything they say.

I see the men swarm around

The piano as she plays.

One-hour snails by,

And the last song is sung.

I hope I can finally talk to her

Now her show is done.

The men stay put.

Much to my displeasure.

I wait for them to get bored.

It seems to take forever.

*'Time to go'*, my sister says.

*'Mum will be wondering where we are.'*

I reluctantly agree to walk with them

Even though we do not live far.

The next night is Saturday.

I come same time, same place

But she is not there,
Oh! How I long to see her face.

After the third night,

I ask about her at the bar.

*'Dotty only comes Fridays,*

*Her babysitter is her Mama.'*

'She has kids?'

*'Yep. Four at home, all boys.*

*No husband to speak of,*

*It's nice she can do something she enjoys.'*

I am in shock.

She looked so young,

Am I ready to be a dad?

I already know I love her,

Could four boys be that bad?

I decide no, I will come on Friday,

Declare my love and how I feel.
Tell her, I will do anything.
To make my dreams of us real.

Friday comes slowly,
But eventually it's time.
I have waited for the moment
When the fair Dotty will be mine.
I have butterflies in my belly
My attire is smart as can be.
I decide to get there early,
And leave just after tea.

I wait on the table by the piano,
My eyes fixed upon the door.
I wait for Dotty to appear,
My feet tap the sticky floor.
The door opens, in she comes
A vision all in blue
'Sorry I'm late Bill, Mama came later.
I'll try and make it up to you.'
Barman Bill gives her a thumbs up,
Dotty sits upon the stool.
I say, 'Hi, Dotty.' She doesn't respond.
I feel like a fool.

She begins to play a joyful tune,
I stand up and sip my beer.
She looks upon my face,
And seems happy and in good cheer.
I start to talk to her,
Between the songs she sings.
I tell her I have fallen in love,
And the joy and hope that brings.
Facing the music sheets,
She again does not respond.
Just ignores me completely,
I feel I have been wronged.
How can she treat me like this?
Not even acknowledge my presence.
How have I offended her?
I bared my heart to silence.
I drop my glass on the bar.
Empty, feeling worthless and bereft.
'I guess I'm not her type.' I tell Bill.
*'Do you not realise she's deaf?'*

Oh, my beautiful Dotty,
You never heard my voice.
When you ignored my advances
It wasn't through your choice.

I look to Bill and ask,

'How do I communicate? Any tips?'

Bill says, *'You need to get her to look at you,*

*She's good at reading lips.'*

So, I walk back and sit down,

As close to Dotty as I can be.

On her break, I touch her arm

She turns and looks at me.

I tell her how much I love her,

And describe her with such beauty.

Dotty looks at me puzzled,

*'Ye can't be talking about me!*

*I am a piano girl, just like any other.*

*When I can't be here, singing away,*

*I am a full-time mother.'*

Dotty gives me a smile

And says *'Now, be on your way.*

*But thank you for the nice compliments.*

*You really made my day.*

*I need to finish my set,*

*My punters are waiting.*

*Music is my life my boy,*

*And my joy is entertaining!'*

I take her rejection as well as I can

And leave without a fight.

Sad and disappointed, I walk home,

As Dotty sings merrily into the night.

# EXCLUSIVE!

## PM DECLARES LAW ABOLISHED AFTER MOTORWAY TRAGEDY OF DOTING FATHERS

Darren Way

British Prime Minister Lydia Black has abolished the famous 'Mothers First' law that she brought in during her first term serving as Prime Minister. After a Mirror journalist exposed her motives as selfish and insincere, she has had no choice but to act. The Mirror exclusive also revealed details about her secret marriage and bribery towards MPs to push the law through the Houses of Parliament.

This has added to the tremendous public pressure to reconsider the law after the tragedy that took 19 lives last week on the M5. 'Mothers First' which gave sole custody to mothers automatically without any unsupervised visitation with the father during divorce proceedings, was met under great criticism from the start as being massively flawed. It was dubbed shocking and inhumane from the public and now it has been revealed Ms Black bribed several members of parliament to push it through and vote in her favour.

Doting fathers immediately took to the streets as the law came into play. Many attempts for a law change went unnoticed as well as petitions compiled of hundreds of thousands of signatures. Desperate fathers declared war on the government and the protests got bigger and bolder. Many camped outside Ms Black's house in Kensington with signs, throwing eggs, slime, and flour. Ms Black called the police, resulting in eight arrests but all were released with just a warning. Calling themselves 'Fathers Unite', the fathers kept coming and Ms Black could not go in and out of her home without being tormented, ridiculed, and spat on.

The protests became more extreme when one incident involved a suspected bomb threat when a box got delivered to Ms Black's private residence. She called the bomb squad, who opened the package to a lifelike doll of a new-born baby with the word 'surplus' painted in red over half of it.

The Mothers First law became a massive talking point worldwide after a YouTube channel started broadcasting videos of young children begging the Prime Minister to change her mind so they could "stay with Daddy." Influencers began their campaign with celebrity fathers wearing t-shirts and declaring their support and admiration for fathers who are fighting for their rights. Instagram sensation Malina Moore described protests as "The Path to Paternal Liberation!" which became the slogan for the 'Fathers Unite' movement.

In a leaked email, Ms Black told her advisers she had had enough of these "arrogant b$*tards" and "had a plan to make them look bad." She didn't think they "had the guts to make a real move." So, she was going to "force their hand".

Ms Black held a press conference to say, "I am tired of these childish taunts and games. I dare all of you Fathers Unite to show you are serious about your children. Show your commitment to your children by really showing me the passion you say you have." Ms Black finished with the statement that will haunt her for the rest of her career. "You say you would die for your children. Prove it."

The fathers took her words literally and a mass of hundreds descended onto the bridge on the M5 threatening to take their own lives for their children. As more piled onto the bridge, fathers started to fall as they were being pushed over to make room, others were crushed under the number of people on the bridge.

Ms Black's true intentions came to light the day after. She was secretly married before and her husband had sole custody of their daughter. It was obvious there was only one solution on the table, the law had to be scrapped. The secret husband and daughter were confirmed to be in witness protection yesterday at 17:01. Ms Black declared the 'Mothers First' law would be abolished and "the custody of children in a separation or divorce would again be decided based on each case."

Among the 19 victims of the M5 tragedy were 7 fathers who were in happy committed relationships but believed in a father's right for fair custody of his children.

One such man was Daniel Hargraves, 29, from Sussex. In an interview on the bridge, he said, "I am lucky enough to see my children every day. Some men are not so lucky and have to fight for that right. This law takes away hope that they might win. My worst nightmare is not seeing my children. Our Prime Minister needs to realise, it's not just the fathers she's hurting but more importantly our children." These are thought to be his last words.

It is a bittersweet victory for 'Fathers Unite' after so many lives were lost and already ruined from a law that only seemed focused on revenge. Twenty-six custody cases had been ruled upon in Britain under the 'Mothers First' law and are under appeal. It is clear Ms Black's resignation is imminent, and a new party leader will soon be announced. It is a high price to pay for revenge against a husband she will never see and a daughter she will never have.

## **THE OPPORTUNITY**

A woman appears from the clearing in the woods and follows the path down the slope. The sun beats down in breaks of trees and light rays burst through its branches. She has benefitted from the summer weather that has come before, her dark brown hair cascades down the middle of her brown shoulders.

Although in wellies, she wears a long summer dress with a split right up to the top of her thigh. Her long brown leg flashes with every step, encouraging a lingering look. Thin spaghetti straps divide her toned shoulders. The blades defined so pleasantly suggesting a slender smooth back inviting you to touch.

Her body moves like fluid, elegance, and grace, she is tall but feminine. Her delicate beauty contrasts with her womanly curves.

Around the corner, there is a winding path, and she disappears. Then, a vision once more. There is a pool of mud. She hitches her dress and holds it bunched on the side. It shows the beauty of both her smooth tanned legs as they move among the dirt. She is careful and takes it slow. Her body improves with every motion. She drops her dress, and again it outlines her smooth silhouette.

The trail appears in waves and she is missed until she is visible again. Intruders come along violating her personal space.

'Good afternoon,' the trespassers say.

She gives a small, gentle smile in return.

The track is rocky amongst the trees and a small brook plays beside her.

A turn of the head to admire nature at its most beautiful. It gives me a chance to admire her in return, another case of nature at its most striking.

A noise.

She turns. I see her face for the first time. Her red lips are full of glamour and beauty. Smooth, generous breasts complete her form. Her big dark brown eyes the same colour as her hair. I feel like I could do so much with those eyes. Watch them react to me and widen, see if she is as transfixed with me as I am with her.

My intended stands motionless, as if suddenly aware of my presence. The trunk I am behind is large and conceals me well. I am sure she cannot see me. The leaves on the trees dance and flutter, a small wind incites a display of rustles.

She turns again and walks a little. To be sure I will not be discovered, I stay put. Sure enough, she looks again. A quicker glance, a simple check.

A family are coming now, and I need to decide what to do. She can see quite a bit of the path behind; she knows there is no one walking directly after her. The children are playing soldiers and running around the trees. I need to decide. Risk being found by some brat or pretend I was looking for something and take the chance she will find out I've been following her.

I take my chances with the brat and cling to the tree. I can hear her voice exchanging pleasantries and small talk with the family about the weather or some other useless information that everyone will forget half an hour later. The kids are getting closer and the mum and dad are laughing on the path. She will be out of sight by now. I cling to the tree.

'Thomas! Henry! Get down from there!'

Thank God.

'Sorry mum!'

The boys go down to the path and join their parents. I try not to make a sound until I know they have passed. I hope I have not lost her, my enchanting creature.

Finally, it feels like enough time has gone past and I re-join the path. She is out of sight. I walk briskly trying to catch her up. A glimpse of a lock of dark hair disappears around the corner. She is close. I turn the corner and I spot her taking an unexpected turn into an area of woodland off the designated path. Maybe she knows I am behind her, maybe this is a signal she wants this too. That isn't what I usually look for, but she is enough of a beauty for me not care. Clever girl. Seduce me, tease me, show me how badly you want it.

She follows a string of a path up to a lane covered by a canopy of trees. The perfect place for us to be together.

'FREDDIE!' she calls without warning.

A boy about 18, is laughing and sitting on a stile.

'Mum!'

She is walking faster now and laughing. I stop. She is not alone. How many more of them are there? It is too much of a risk for us to be together. I must leave her and my prospects of our time together behind. She is a fraud, full of duplicity. I am angry and have rapid thoughts about taking care of them both, but she is impure and not worth the effort.

I take another small path away. I must find a place to wait. Another opportunity will come along soon. I guarantee it.

# NEW YEAR CONFESSIONS

'You've got to do it, Jess. You broke up with Ryan, now it's time to take the next step.' Rachel bit into her biscuit as she rested her mug of tea on her mountainous belly. She turned to her sister, 'you did this because you wanted a new start. Don't chicken out now.'

Jess exhaled a long breath. 'All right, I'll text him.'

Two streets away, a phone pinged with Jess's message asking to meet up at the park in an hour. It was read and placed on the arm of the sofa. Two friends tapped their thumbs and fingers ferociously as they tried to defeat and kill everyone they encountered on the screen.

'I'm going to tell Jess how I feel today, mate.'

Wade carried on staring at the television, ' I thought she was with Ryan?'

Lee killed another soldier, 'Nah, broke up last week. I should have told her the first time before she got with him. I don't want to miss my chance again.'

'She wants to meet up in an hour.'

Lee dropped his controller, 'really? Shit, today? Okay.'


An hour later, Wade and Lee were sat on a bench close to the swings. Neither of the boys could sit still. Lee got up, retied his hair back into a ponytail and zipped up his jacket.

Wade took a deep breath and stood up to face him, 'Lee, I have something I need to tell you. I think it's probably best to tell you while you're distracted. That way it won't be so …mega I guess.'

Lee paced about, not able to stand still. 'What is it? Tell me now before she gets here.'

'Well, I wanted to say it before we go back to school. It's kind of difficult. You see...'

Before Wade could say anymore, Jess appeared at the gate.

'Lee! I wasn't expecting to see you!' Jess glared at Wade who looked just as uncomfortable as her. His long sandy hair draped over his eyes. Jess straightened her denim skirt, suddenly conscious of the effort she made.

'You look nice Jess. I love it when you wear your hair down like that.' Lee stared at his feet, 'did you have a good Christmas? Has Rachel had the baby yet?'

Jess looked at Wade for guidance, but he seemed to be avoiding her gaze. 'Umm ...no. It's a couple of weeks over now, so Rachel's a bit fed up. Christmas was cool. I got the GHDs I wanted.'

Lee smiled, 'cool.'

Jess stepped forward, 'listen, I need to tell Wade something. It's important. Do you mind Lee?'

Lee chewed his cheek, 'I guess. I kind of need to tell you something too. Something I kinda wanted to say for ages.'

'What is it? What do you need to tell me?' Jess preferred to just get hers over with so her and Wade could talk. However, she knew Lee well enough to know the best way to get rid of him was to let him have his say.

Lee moved towards her.

'Are you okay with Wade hearing this?' Jess asked him.

'Wade knows.'

'Oh, okay.'

Lee put his hand through his hair, 'you see the thing is Jess, I like you. I have done for a long time actually.'

Jess took a step back, 'but I like Wade! That's why I dumped Ryan.'

Lee and Jess stared at Wade.

'Say something Wade for god's sake!' Jess pleaded irritably.

Wade stared at them both back, his moment had come.

'I'm gay.'

# **LOVE**

Love is the most beautiful thing in the world. It is what we are here for. We were born to love; from our first breath, we search for it. The love in a mother and fathers' eyes, bathing in the comfort that brings. It's what we need to make our life safe. Whole.

We grow and we experience love in a new form, romantic love; that's when our lives seem to begin. The look. From one lover's eyes to another. The warmth of their entire being, their soul connecting with yours. We relish it, search for it on screen or in a song so we can relive it day after day. We can't get enough. The feeling when someone loves you like that, and you feel the same way shows you how wondrous love can be.

The first time your lips touch, you drift into this abyss and the world you knew disappears. The only place you want to be is with them, being apart tortures your mind and you see them in everything you see and touch.

You may get married. Your wedding day is like a dream, it's what you imagined over and over in your mind. Everyone around you is happy, friends, relatives, share the joy in your moments that are treasured for years to come.

You may create life out of love. And then the one you fell so deeply for sees you in a new light. You are what the child needs. You are who it searches for in that first breath. You provide the comfort, the safety and make their world whole. It is a gift. Every time you look at that child you are overwhelmed with the capacity your heart can feel.

The person you fell in love with gives you fewer looks, and you do likewise with them. Romance dulls. Now and again, you see it. They take a moment to look at you because they cannot help it. Pleasure becomes more of being together. Sharing moments, making each other laugh, doing little things for each other that felt so irrelevant in the early days but now show romance and thoughtfulness.

After the children grow, you have time again together with added visitors. Your children fall in love, create a life of their own that you share with them. You refresh, find new ways to be together, to fall in love.

Then the inevitable. One day they are gone. Your world is torn apart, the life you built. So, knowing the heartache and unbearable pain that will surely come. Is it worth it? The torture?

I say yes! To live is to love.

Love will cause pain. All those moments bring joy, before and after that inevitable day. And when you are loved, truly loved, with the whole soul of another being; it is magical. Momentous. Breathtaking. And worth every future tear.

# THE CHAMELEON

One day he is kind

One day he is cruel

He treats his lovers like queens

He treats them as fools.

He tries to help strangers

Polite throughout his day

He will call his father names

And push his mother away.

He flirts for his ego

Full to the brim with self-pride

He gets defensive

Struggling inside.

He treats people well

Lots of flowers he sends

But his cupboards are bare

He borrows money from his friends.

Some days he looks well

Laughing at jokes he makes

Other days he won't shave

And his hands start to shake.

He does his job well

He barely rests or sits

Eyes darting everywhere

Looking forward to his next hit.

A Christmas Box is something you fill with seasonal food and surprises so a family in need can still celebrate Christmas and enjoy the festive season. I thought it would be nice to include something personal and different, so I wrote a story called The Christmas Bus for them to share in case their hard times had lasted more than one year. Christmas box appeals take place all over the UK, and the scheme really helps others. More information can be found online, but I recommend including things such as pictures the children have drawn or homemade ornaments, just to give the families something a little extra special.

One Christmas Eve, when the stars beamed and the air was crisp, the pavement glistened as a long forest green bus made its one stop that night. The lengthy line of passengers boarded and took seats on luxurious deep red velvet chairs faced toward each other. Holly lined the windows signifying eternal life and magical times, and bountiful decorations of red, white, and pink poinsettias adorned the roof bringing wishes of mirth and celebration.

Every passenger on board felt they were missing something. Some had empty stomachs, some lost loved ones or family, some ached for their youth, some were without self-worth or any joy in their hearts.

As their trip began and the bus moved, the scenery changed gradually from the world and life they knew to frosted trees, crystallised droplets of rain and a sky of rich arctic and midnight blue. Shooting stars soared through the night, inviting wishes to be made for those with hope.

Everything was shared during the journey. Memories were recounted of loved ones passed, keeping them alive in the hearts that missed them. Everyone drank and ate happily, filling bellies long empty. Others watched the children, making themselves feel young, feeling nostalgia about their own Christmases past.

Carols were sung with vigour and friendships were made. Everyone showed each other love and respect as they rejoiced in the festive season. People listened to each other. Every stranger, young or old felt important and needed. Each passenger learnt they had valuable gifts that meant so much to so many. The clock slowed to allow these changes to grow and enrich the lives of the passengers. It gave them hope that there was so much more to appreciate within themselves and the world around them.

The Christmas Bus made them realise everyone feels like they are missing something important in their lives, it may be something they need, or forced to live without. But when people come together, even strangers, and share their good fortune, they become whole and want for nothing.

This is the magic of Christmas. It is within our power to make enchantments happen, especially for one another. We are all passengers, learning how miraculous the journey of life can be. Especially when we take the ride together.

# WEATHER

**Wind**

The wind howls through the trees, I sit outside, my hair blowing across and away from my face. It feels fresh but aggressive. The invisible intruder lifts my dress and blows on my legs. The sun fights to show through to warm the world beneath but the wind is strong. The blades of grass dance on the lawn and the bushes and flowers sway around it. Now and again a burst of wind hits and I feel the energy and force. It tries to test me, but I am also strong and can withhold its gust.

    The trees bend and rustle, they whisper to each other a warning that the air is angry, bellowing its thrust and determined sense of will. The clouds move slowly as if unaffected and above the actions of the wind. As if they are parents waiting out a tantrum.

    People's coats flutter like hero's capes, children theatrically hold on to their mother, trying not to fly up in the air and blow away. Now and again the wind screams to be heard, demands it. Hear me. Feel my strength. Trust in my power. I can move you. I can move things around you.

    A garden chair blows across the patio stones, clipping its leg against the wall. A playhouse suffers the blustery wrath and crashes across the garden, tumbling like a prop from *The Wizard of Oz*.

Birds fight to fly across the sky and stay on course, not knowing whether they will make it back to their nest. Field animals run into holes in the grass for shelter. Cars sway slightly, lifted by the force of the wind. Drivers rush to get home, trying to be safe inside their dwelling.

**Rain**

People hear it before they see it, its downpour becomes lines of broken flickers almost invisible to the human eye. It glistens the world making the ground squelch and slippery paths to be wary of. It can make people scream and run as it plummets making its entrance. Yet children laugh with glee as they don their hats and play in boots stamping in dips the rain has filled.

Sometimes it is gentle, people hardly notice the drizzle as it shimmers their hair. Lovers kiss, feeling the droplets caress their face as their lips meet. As the rain touches the hard ground, the water dances creating a magical show for those with imagination and a dreamy outlook on the world around them.

The rain feeds nature and provides much-needed refreshment for the wildlife and crops in the field nourishing the harvest. Farmers pray for this act, relief from the dehydrating sun. The clouds cleanse and feed the world. They help the world thrive and reminisce of days gone by. Memories of childhood and loved ones long passed.

The droplets crawl down the window, giving the glass natural sparkle and splattered patterns to watch come alive and change seconds after the first touch.

The rain creates a danger to those at sea and wild swimmers, entering at their peril, or surviving the elements as best they can. It has many stages but also many uses and as well as watching in awe, we watch with admiration, disappointment, laughter, and indifference.

## Sunshine

Shoulders burn as they expose themselves to its rays. A flawless blue above heads, and white patterns waiting for imagination to take hold and breathe new adventures into their design.

A mower in the background, a gentle breeze brings relief. Skin on show everywhere trying to go brown. Children play happily, their legs and arms bare covered in creamy lotion.

Families bundle into cars determined to make the most of the day. Most are headed to the sea; a natural calling of nostalgia and perfect days lures them to the shores.

Arrays of washing across the nation lined up in a row, microwaving slowly in the tepid glow.

The day is described as beautiful, glorious, and gorgeous. The preferred outcome to each new day and the most appreciated and relished. This is the weather that makes a huge difference to temperance and moods, everyone is happier, eager to laze, eager to move around and explore.

People pray for the sun to shine its light on their most important days and breaks from their routine in new worlds and surroundings. Cameras are the ultimate accessory as everything bathes in golden glow. The sun's full glare forces bodies to glisten and become wet and sticky.

## Snow and ice

A density contradiction of powder and cold hardness. A bringer of joy and danger. Thoughtlessly creating chaos in its path, unforgiving hazards, pausing lives of all who live around them.

The excitement and laughter when the snow begins to fall, children play, create, and slide. Their parents enjoy watching the happiness in their child's face but are wary of the peril and distress this seemingly magical world can bring. Cars transform from an essential tool to a standstill, an invitation of jeopardy and chance.

Nature freezes and becomes cold and brittle. The ground crunches beneath heavy feet as the world becomes a glittery array of sparkle and life paused in time. Animals struggle to remain safe and warm, to feed their young and survive.

It's piercing cool biting air overtakes the senses, chilling and nipping at uncovered skin. Bitter raw hostile bursts of breeze attack life, and show how helpless and vulnerable we are to the most unforgiving element.  We are at nature's mercy and must react and cope as best we can.


Weather is so ordinary, yet it is the basis for everything we need to survive. Food, shelter, body temperature, water, everything is subject to the elements. It is the most powerful thing in our world that can destroy lives, but also romanticise and enrich them.  Each day we have, every plan we make, is dependent on the skies.

We are all vulnerable to its power and so is everything around us.

# THINGS I LEARNT
# AS A MUM- TOP TIPS!

**\*Coffee is a gift from the Gods. Treasure it always.**

I can't remember drinking much coffee before I became pregnant with my firstborn, but at some point, along the way, it became my closest friend. I always insist on my favourite brand being stocked as there is nothing worse than crappy coffee. You do not want to speak to me before coffee. Do you think PMT is bad? It's nothing compared to a bit of morning small talk with no caffeine. Best impression of Maleficent losing it at the party she wasn't invited to. Class. A. Bitch. With frizzy hair. And pyjamas.

Whenever I am meeting a friend it is always for coffee as we both know its glorious power. And cake. If you don't have a cake, it's weird. I look at those poor souls in Costa and Starbucks who just have paninis. Or worse, oversized cups with only a saucer for company.

You can always tell the newbies to coffee. They are the ones who order the syrup that you treat yourself to at Christmas when you have gingerbread latte. Let's face it, at Christmas, as much gingerbread and cinnamon flavouring as you can pile into everything the better. Food, drink, room spray, the tree, the bathroom, your husband's pants, the list goes on. It's the scent of the season!

But to order a Caramel Latte in June? Such a beginner's move. In time you choose Americano, Cappuccino or Latte. Most bounce around those three, but you always have one you prefer above all others. Mine is the Cappuccino. Bring on the foam and don't forget the chocolate sprinkles! I love it. If I see it and I can't have it, I feel a little downhearted.

So, if you are new to motherhood get ready to make a new best friend you can't live without. And don't forget to grab every loyalty coffee card from every place you visit. Nothing is sweeter when you get to spend time with your favourite best friend for free.


**\*Picking up after my children is half my day, don't waste energy moaning about it, because they don't care**

Kids will play and leave. They are completely oblivious that anyone puts the toy away after it hasn't moved for an hour. Each has the memory of a -goldfish and are distracted by everything, which is why toilet training is so much fun (groan). This belief that things magically disappear also goes for food wrappers. With little scrumptious snack monsters, there are so many wrappers Oscar the Grouch could fill his can in a day. Maybe even his summer garbage can too.

(And don't believe Janet when she says her kids don't snack. She may give them raisins in front of you, but it's only because she promised them a Maccy's Happy Meal on the way home.)


**\*Crisps are children's version of Coffee. Accept it, it makes it so much easier than arguing every 5 seconds, and they WILL keep asking EVERY 5 BLOODY SECONDS!!!!**

Kids are obsessed with crisps. They will have a lunchbox at a café just because they have nice crisps and then they will only eat the packet of crisps. Which makes the crisps about £4. This is especially infuriating when you get them one at a supermarket café and they use their own brand. You know you can get a packet of 6 of them yards away from the shelf for 85p.

Sometimes you get away with blackmailing, eat this before you can have crisps but that doesn't always work. When you buy more crisps, (literally every other day) the kids will eat more of them as they are excited by the sheer number of packets and believe it is party time!

The only time when they will not touch them is when a packet is stuck to the bag of packaging. Default crisps. Those are smelly and filled with poo apparently. Otherwise, they disappear faster than a bottle of prosecco in a room full of women on a night out.

**\*A drawing of a circle with random lines will make you cry.**

The circle is misshapen, the lines are all over the place, it has one shoe, one eye and a giant hand but your kid's self-portrait will get you reaching for the tissues every time. Try not to show it to others, they do not care that your child sees itself as a deformed version of Forky from Toy Story.

Unless of course, you show it to the Grandparents; they love anything. If they leave a pen lying on paper and it makes a dot, they will think the kid's a genius. 'He's drawn the moon! Hey, maybe our little fella will grow up and become an astronaut!' Yep, watch out NASA, the kid doesn't know what a planet is, and thinks an empty kitchen roll is a rocket but I am sure he will blow you away.

**\*Wet wipes are the greatest invention on earth, never be without them!**

They clean everything! Faces, shoes, the bathroom, clothes, you can put unfinished food in them and wrap them up, they are a hand cleaner, makeup remover, duster. The list goes on! Once you discover them, you never go back. Stock up, as the panic when you can't find them is worse than losing your keys.

**\*Always keep the necessities close by.**

Wine. A glass. A corkscrew.

**\*There will be a time when you will learn to accept your body completely.**

Yes, there will always be bits you want to change, but at some point, you will simply think, *I don't mind anymore.*

Most ladies' bodies go to pot the moment they get knocked-up. A few go back to size 8 jeans, but even then, there are very few that are back to pre-mama-bikini-ready-bods. The good news is, once you reach a certain point of, *I don't mind* and mean it, you relax, and your personality shines through. This is the time when you become your most brilliant. You have a laugh and embarrass your children (sometimes on purpose- so much fun. Payback at last for all those tantrums as a toddler. Sometimes not on purpose- and you cringe even yourself).

Some try an exercise class once a week (others don't bother as 5 seconds on a mini trampoline has them rushing to the loo). Others follow beautiful people on reality shows like 'love island' and just enjoy watching their kids grow. Which is the best bit. Watching them grow. And the baby smell. I miss the baby smell.

**\*The toilet will never again be private. Accept this early on.**

Whether you like it or not, the chances are, as soon as your baby can climb stairs, you will never pee alone unless they are asleep or at school. Believe me, you take the time to appreciate those.

Unfortunately, you do get rather used to leaving the door open, and your husbands default move as he ventures up the stairs is to avert his eyes. There are only so many times he can witness you watching 'Friends' on your phone whilst doing a poo. Who says romance is dead?

In the beginning, though, you do lock the door. But you soon learn. You will hear fighting, questionable noises, crying, screaming or worse. Complete silence.

You waddle to the door, (depending on the noise, you might fall over trying to get there in time) and holler downstairs. The first time you do it, the chances are your baby can hardly talk, but you live in hope that in the last two and a half minutes that is no longer an issue, and their vocabulary has improved three times over.

The more kids you have, the better your hollering gets, and you develop amazing skills at identifying mystery noises from 100 feet away- one level up. Your privacy is non-existent, and the door is wide open.

Like I say, it's a strange habit to break. Many a time I have forgotten we had visitors and my pee must have echoed down the stairs. I realise, think I hear a noise, and hold a hand-towel to cover me while I waddle like I'm performing a magician's trick (minus the levitating balls).

One phrase that always pops up is, 'Don't make me come down there!' which, let's face it, is highly improbable unless dinosaurs broke in and threatened to eat your children. And even then, you'd be tempted to give them a head start.

**\*Chicken nuggets, cereal and pizza are the only things that stop my children looking like something from the third world. Feed them what you can get away with without them becoming obese.**

I have tried Jo Frost, Eat Well for Less, and every other TV advice or theory you can think of. "Only give them the good stuff", "disguise veg", "just say no". I tried that. Do you know what happened? They starved themselves until I gave in. Not one evening, two. Two and a half days they only drank water and so I relented. Stubborn mini mind-taunters!

The good stuff goes on their plates, but they don't touch it. Did as babies, ate everything, then somehow along the way, they had a change of heart. We compromise now and they have vitamins. Most kids are the same. I don't worry about it now, I'm sure they'll grow out of it. Won't they?

**\*The Ick factor will disappear**

When you start on the journey of motherhood, you imagine it will all be wonderful. Admiring glances, perfect skin, baby soft hair, dressing them up in cute little outfits, tiny booties poking out of adorable little feet. Pretty soon you are knocked down to earth with tar nappies, projectile vomiting and a baby that poos upwards.

The ick factor present at the start of motherhood disappears rapidly. You are ready for anything and it won't bother you. Vomit, wee on you, poo on you, paint, food, clearing up questionable stains on beds, fear of creepy crawlies is conquered, you turn into a cleaner, exterminator and one of those bio-men the army has for nuclear waste.

And if you get to go on a rare night out, as much as you try to dodge every obstacle and threat to your nice clothes, something will end up on you. That is the ideal time for the all-powerful wet wipes.

## *Always keep a secret stash of chocolate nearby

There are times when the kids will drive you insane and you feel your energy drain out of you. The quickest way to get it back is chocolate. Picks you up instantly. You must keep it secret though or the little darlings will eat it all. Believe me, I have horror stories that will break your heart more than the ones asking for donations to the Dog fund. Don't worry, your ninja skills develop over time and your moves will be silent.

## *Glitter comes from the devil, be prepared

Kids love glitter. Every parent hates it. It will get everywhere, and I mean everywhere! In their ears, on the carpet, in their hair, even on the television. Every surface within a mile radius of where you are using it will be smothered. And the picture or card you thought they were all working so quietly on will contain half a bottle of glue and two-thirds of the glitter bottle. There will be so much on that one card it will bend unapologetically under the sheer weight of the crap poured over it.

That nice drawing they did that you thought was so well done will have disappeared under a red, gold, or silvery mass. On the bright side, younger children end up in a great mood as they believe they have evolved into unicorns after having a string of sparkly poos.

## *Don't rely on Dad, he has hidden powers that make him invisible to younglings

No matter where you are (a floor away), and no matter where he is (usually sat beside your children). Your offspring would rather go on an expedition to find you than ask their father. Even the simple things or a request (normally asking for crisps), he will turn on those magic powers and become invisible. Your children would rather you journey back and forth all over the place, stop having that poo, cease ironing or making beds, to ask you. Even when there's one minute on the timer in the kitchen, they need you to watch something random than ask the grownup next to them to see their interpretive dance of a strawberry plant.

The superpower is so intense, the kid could be sitting on the man's lap and the child will still stop, not see him and find you: the mum. Nothing you can do will stop it. I have marched my children, lined them up and introduced them to the man who's been living with us since the beginning of their birth. I have played the one-option game of 'Guess Who?', with my sons and daughter begging them to acknowledge this man is also available to take care of their needs. Yet still, they are blind to him!

## *Get ready for Christmas to get real

One of the best things about kids is Christmas. It goes into another dimension. All the magic and innocence return, along with hefty price tags. Even if you don't blow out on presents, you will spend out on all the stuff leading up to it. So, start saving now.

Pantos, school functions, coffees, and catchups with every other person with kids to exchange presents. Hopefully, by now you have a present box where stuff is reduced to virtually nothing and looks more expensive than it is. Absolute godsend. And once you've been caught out with a classmate's birthday, a card box will appear too. Then you have local Christmas markets (only posh people go abroad for them), parades (whatever faith you have with humanity will vanish over who can stand closest to the metal barrier), and of course, grottos.

Oh, the grottos! You think your kid will be excited to see the big man in red, but in truth, they are petrified and very rarely have any idea what to say. All you want is a photo and no matter how many fake beards and uncomfortable poses you acquire other the years, you still do it. No one knows why, it is just the law. Along with baking with kids. You must bake something and they 'help'. The classic must be the gingerbread house.

Oh, the gingerbread house! What a bloody nightmare! First, you create stencils. No idea. Printed them out online, very much like when you made boxes out of card at school and you did the nets. Remember the nets? With tabs? And you always cut a tab off, swear, get told off by the teacher for bad language and in the end stick it together with tape and it looked like it had already been through the recycling bin.

You make the dough for gingerbread, you either add too much ginger or not enough. One will taste like cardboard and the other will taste like spicy cardboard. Roll it out, and cut out the stencil. Then you put it in the oven where it loses all the shape of the stencil, and you already know you're done for.

Icing is meant to glue it together, but I have not found this. Mine does not stick together. Instead, I resort to gentle leaning and a strong sense of balance. But hey! Then you get to decorate it!

In your mind, there is an image of a beautiful house straight out of a storybook. And maybe if you were experienced this could happen. Instead, due to the leaning, I must pour icing over the side and throw silver balls at it hoping some will stick.

What does come in handy is that emergency bag of Haribo you keep at the back of the cupboard. Throw some of that on, nothing says Christmas like fried eggs and a cola bottle.

Of course, by the time you have finished, no one wants to eat it. You can tell yourself it's because no one wants to spoil the illusion of the pretty little house from Hansel and Gretel, but the reality is no matter how many days the gingerbread house has been constructed, it still looks sticky and frankly a bit gross.

*And finally…*

**\*Advice is bullcrap.**

Everyone does it differently, every tactic is acceptable. If you only remember one thing, remember that. Each to their own. To be honest, none of us has a clue! It's a jungle. Stop caring, enjoy what you can and keep coffee, chocolate, and alcohol in ready supply. It's every parent for themselves!

# THE GIRL WITH THE GOLDEN HAIR

I once knew a girl with hair as golden as the sun.

The warmth radiated from her locks,
Even after darkness had come.

The waves floated down her back
And flowed without care,
The wind gracefully caressing her curls
Delicately rising in the air.

Sunlight's rays
Illuminating every distinct strand.
Glorious and dazzling.
An amplification of glistening sand.

Mesmerised,
I can only watch in awe.
I wondered if she realised
The serenity of her shimmering glow,
So beautiful and pure.

I saw this girl day by day,

Envying her style.

But if you thought her hair took your breath away

You should have seen her when she smiled.

 For Jaime.

# WOMAN SOLDIER

I grab my gun from under the shelf
The bullets get loaded, I taught myself
I kiss my mama and papa goodbye
And I tell myself not to cry.

I see crowds gather as I get outside
Deserters now have nowhere to hide
My hair is cut to resemble a man
Bravery is my mask since my duty began.

My body is covered, so not to entice
We are taught to shoot, not to warn twice
We patrol the streets, with menace and severity
Making sure people know, this is our territory.

My family is safe if I play my part
No one can touch them or tear us apart.
We will remain together, like only a few
If others want that assurance, they change into a soldier too.

We investigate a home, together we ransack
I'm scared a life will be taken we can never give back.
They think the man is a traitor, not one of us
The mother promises their virtue, that they won't cause a fuss.

The baby is crying. A boy my age, not yet sixteen
He does not react, to anything he has seen
They have trained him well, be silent, stay still
The soldiers will remain calm, they will not shoot to kill.

He knows I have no choice,
I will do what needs to be done
My career embodied with captivity
has only just begun.

# **SELF SERVICE**

Belle entered the supermarket and pushed her trolley to the side of the lobby. After a good rummage in her handbag, she found her list and purse in the zipped compartment and took out her loyalty card. The handheld scanners were on the wall, she strolled over and placed the card under the flashing infrared line. A handset lit up inviting Belle to take it. Resting it in the hole provided on the trolley, she took her usual route and read her list again to try and remember as much as she could. The trip was going well until she came to the eggs. For some reason, the barcode wouldn't scan. After several attempts, and trying the codes on three other boxes, she got annoyed and put them in the trolley anyway. She was about to scan a multipack of chocolate bars which were roughly the same price but then she thought no. It's the store's fault the item won't scan, the store will have to take the hit. Such was Belle's determination to teach the store a lesson that when the message appeared with the question Did everything scan? She hit Yes, took her receipt, and walked out.

      Belle was ready to be stopped at the doors, and she had an argument ready and waiting. It was the store's incompetence that made her do it. As she walked out of the store, she stopped to see if anyone was following her, but strangely everything seemed normal. No one was rushing out or trying to catch her. Now she was stuck. What should she do? Belle walked to her car, opened her boot, and packed in the shopping. Then she drove home. On her journey home she thought it shouldn't be this easy should it?

The next weekend the store was insanely busy, Belle could hardly move in the aisles. The tills were packed. She used self-service again but this time she consciously put a box of expensive chocolate truffles in the trolley without scanning to see if she could get away with it. There was enough cash in her purse to plead ignorance if she got caught. Her hands were damp with sweat as Belle clung to the trolley handle for courage. With her heart was beating ferociously through her chest, and mindful of attracting attention, she approached the self-service checkout.    Avoiding eye contact, and with her head down, Belle scanned the barcode to bring up her shopping on the screen. A clang cut through the background noise of other customers, making Belle jump.

'Excuse me, you dropped this,' a man said standing in front of her holding a tin of sweetcorn.

Belle forced a smile, 'thank you.'

The man smiled back and resumed his own transaction on his till.

A message flashed on the screen. Did everything scan?

After a moments pause, Belle pressed yes and proceeded to the payment screen. After using her card, she pushed her trolley along the shop floor to the exit. Again, she was not stopped. Belle got out of the store and a rush of energy ran through her body. She had got away with it.

A week later she had her children with her, and they came to the magazine aisle. The children started asking for a magazine. Belle wondered whether to try again, only with something bigger this time. She chose a magazine for each and hid them under her bag in the trolley seat. After re-arranging her bag, the magazines were covered completely. This time she went through the till with a cashier. If she got found out she could claim forgetfulness because the kids kept playing up. She got through the till, paid with cash and her bag didn't move.

Belle walked out to the car and put the kids in their car seats. She packed away the shopping leaving her bag for last. A member of staff was coming her way wearing a luminous vest. Belle froze, unsure of what to do. He was getting closer. She could feel her heart beating so fast, it was coming out of her chest. He was still headed towards her.

'Oh God,' Belle said underneath her breath, 'please, God, I'll stop. Please don't let me get caught. Please, God, not with my children here. Please, God. Please!'

The man passed her and went to the trolley park situated beside her car.

That was close. Thank you, God, thought Belle. I shall never do this again.

She drove home, but again a rush of energy thrilled her, and she felt dangerous, devilish, and excited. She had got away with it. Again. The fear had vanished along with the memory of the statement she made, and she tried taking more the following week. Every week she tried again. She knew she should stop but justified it by only taking small things she could afford to pay for.

Sometimes, they needed to do a random check. On one occasion, she was lucky she chose to be good that day and the check went through without a problem. On another check, they scanned three random items which happened to be items she scanned. But one time she had her kids with her, and two items weren't accounted for. The staff member told her she would now have to check everything. Belle told them off for putting things in the trolley, pretending to be horrified and outraged. She also blamed them for not scanning everything as she had let them do it as a treat. Five items had to be paid for separately. The member of staff asked her coolly if she could make sure she was the only one to scan in future. Riddled with guilt, Belle agreed and bought the children fish and chips on the way home.

Finally, she did get caught and Belle was alone when it happened. She protested the item hadn't scanned and she pressed the wrong button. Her whole face went red, she could feel the embarrassment, judgement and shame overwhelm her. She felt like the member of staff knew she did it on purpose and that was when Belle stopped. On the way home, she imagined her husband being called by security with the news that his wife had been caught stealing mascara. The makeup she could afford but too reckless to pay for. He had never been arrested and he would never forget what she had done. Belle would bring shame to their family, to her children. She knew people who worked at the supermarket. What if news of her indiscretion travelled throughout her community and the school. Her reputation and that of her family would be sullied, and always talked about.

During her mini crime spree, Belle googled whether members of the public also did this. When it turned out across the world people were stealing, she thought it wasn't so bad. There was even a story of a man trying to pass a PlayStation 4 across as fruit who was jailed and Belle thought as all her items were small, she was a good one. A small fish to the big powerful supermarket, who would not be too upset as the most she had stolen was a £10 paddling pool just to see if she could.

Now she had stopped, Belle was relived. She saw what she did was wrong as the shop had given their customers a position of trust and she had abused it. She stopped self-scanning and only went through tills. She was sure stores stole too from customers when they were vulnerable, such as putting their prices up at Christmas and during summer when they know people will have to buy more, and they get extra footfall. So maybe they abused her trust too.

But, even if they did, Belle realised it was no excuse for taking advantage. She had displayed all the traits of the kind of people she warned her children against. Dishonesty, criminality, deception, treachery, she even knowingly falsely accused her own children at one point to escape blame. The lure to feel that adrenalin again was strong, but the feeling of shame overpowered any temptation she had. Everything Belle had done had involved risk, but each one she took was the same. Unnecessary. Uncalculated. And most importantly, full of regret.

# **THE TELEPHONE**

When you invent something to help mankind and it benefits the world, God allows you to occasionally watch your creation thrive from heaven after you die.
    So, when Alexander Graham Bell died, he was able to watch his invention of the telephone evolve more and more. His drawings of almost funnels were a far cry from the mobile phones he saw people using today. Although it pleased him enormously to see that he was credited with what was categorised in modern years as a necessity, it also irked him how much people had run away with the idea. Phones on watches, in automobiles, people could even call each other just using computers. It was far from what he had in mind when he designed his machine, he wanted to bring people together. Not make it easier for them to stay apart. However, one thing he did see and enjoy was the different ways human lives were enriched by his humble telephone.

A woman spent every day alone without a person to speak to or see her. She was invisible and consumed with loneliness with an empty heart longing to touch another human hand.
    Then, her phone rang, and her son who had not spoken to her in so many years, stuck in another country and culture, said the word we use every day without thought or tactic. 'Hello.'
    She wished she could afford to see him or speak to him as much as she wanted. She missed him terribly, her entire life was devoted to him. When he left, her world drained of colour. All it took was one word to brighten and revitalise her world. And it was thanks to the telephone she got to hear it.

On Christmas Day, three children eagerly opened their presents but, after the initial burst of excitement, the children played with their new toys and their mother watched with sadness and joy in her eyes.

It was the second Christmas he had missed, and the only one the babe in her arms had ever known. She just had to make it till after dinner and she would hear his voice. She wondered what he was eating as she ate her extravagant roast dinner. And whether the mood was chirpy or sombre on the army base. Time dragged but at last, he called. The sensation of hearing his voice felt like a Christmas miracle. She cried when she recognised his easy-going tone on the other end. Her children would hear him too soon enough. The telephone reunited that family on the most magical day of the year and allowed them to be together the only way they could.

But the telephone didn't just bring joy, it brought emotion the other way too. Early morning, a young man received a call. his father was in trouble and not breathing. The neighbour who had the spare key was erratic and panic was in his voice.

'The ambulance men have been here for hours,' the neighbour told him.

They stayed on the phone sometimes talking, sometimes crying, at moments just silently until it was official.

After that phone call, the young man's whole life fell apart and he became a different person.

In Canada in the 1980s, a bored housewife spoke to a telecanvasser who wanted to sell her double glazing. The woman politely declined but somehow the conversation kept going. His voice was familiar and after a long chat, she and the caller realised that they were old lovers from long ago. The phone call continued, and they decided to meet. They began an affair and six months later the housewife left her husband for her lover. An outcome only made possible by the telephone.

In Liverpool, a tall man called Dermot was crouched in the kitchen clutching his arm. His wife had poured boiling water from the kettle over it because he did not have her breakfast ready when she came downstairs. It was his punishment.

269

She punished him frequently, usually two or three times a day. Dermot came from a proud family. He told his father about his wife.

His dad replied, 'toughen up and whack her back! One smack and she'll learn to respect her husband.'

But Dermot could never hit a woman. He never confided in anyone else.

As he held a wet cold cloth over the burn on his forearm, he knew he could not go into work today to operate machinery at the plant. It was hot work, filled with steam and cramped conditions, he would be in agony. Dermot called in sick. He knew he was letting his employer down, along with his workmates. Full of guilt, he decided this could not continue.

Dermot turned on his computer and searched for male domestic abuse and was shocked to find as much as 40% of all abuse cases are male. He was not alone. He found a helpline and took the first step in changing his life and dialled on the home telephone.

For the first time, Dermot told another human being everything she had done to him and disclosed the full extent of the violence and cruelty he had suffered at the hands of his wife. He broke down in tears as he spoke. Dermot got help.

It had been 17 minutes since Matt and Chloe made the offer and the wait was excruciating. They had saved for a deposit, sat down with three mortgage advisors, they had searched for their perfect first home for 15 months. The flat inside a refurbished church was perfect, it had all the character they were looking for but with a modern feel. There were two parking spaces, one for each of them and it even had a bit of a garden.

They could imagine their life there, living together, no longer going from parents' home to parents' home. But they could not afford it. The estate agent hinted there might be a deal to be made as the owner was looking for a quick sale. The sellers had another building to renovate and needed the money tied up within the flats. They had tried 10k lower which was declined, then 8k, again rejected. So now they were at

£7,000 below the asking price. They could not go any higher, if this was turned down as well, they would lose it. The mortgage payments at 7k were going to make things tight, but it was doable.

22 minutes had passed. They would normally go for a walk during stressful times, but they could not leave the house in case they got the call. 36 minutes. They made a cup of tea. 52 minutes. The phone began to ring.

Alexander Graham Bell had watched his invention for almost 100 years. He had seen it evolve, cause heartache, joy, anger, laughter, every emotion a human being could experience could be evoked with one conversation on the telephone. After years of watching others, Alexander realised why God let you watch. When something is created, no matter how inanimate the object, it can bring life and create new beginnings, something without thought or plan can determine a person's life for the better or gravitate it toward the bad.

We have no idea of our impact on a world of strangers or the generations to come.

# Dedicated to Frances

In heaven, there is no judgement.
It's a place where you're loved by all.
A land where you're 'On Top of the World'
Where the righteous do not fall.
Someone always supports you,
You never feel alone.
You know you are always cared for.
In your dreams, you can roam.

You feel completely content
That nothing can scare you away,
You feel the world is your oyster
That there's never enough to say.
Feelings are spoken frequently.
Hope is always felt.
Thoughtfulness is everywhere
'*I love you*' is always meant.

Sometimes I think about Heaven,

But one thing is always clear

Although sometimes it feels so far away

My Heaven is always here.

My heaven is my mum.

# MAIL CRUSH

I think I fancy our postman,

I always want him to wait and chat a while

I wonder if he is on shift today and daydream about his smile.

He's short, but dark and handsome.

With olive skin and deep brown eyes.

When he bends over, I see his bottom and drool at his muscular thighs.

His uniform hardly contains his chest

When I see him, I change position, so I look my best.

When he smiles, there's a set of perfect teeth

I look at his clothes and fantasise what's underneath.

His legs are toned and so refined

I can tell from his attitude with elderly customers, he is also kind.

He begins his route as the day is dawning

To every person he passes, he greets 'Good morning'.

All the single residents use tactics to make him stay,

Wearing next to nothing, enticing him to play.

Our neighbour brings and bakes him cakes

I have no culinary skills or ways to make

Him notice me above others.

And make him want me as his lover.

The competition is fierce, ladies at war!

Every time we see him, he leaves us wanting more.

But there is just one thing that blows my crush apart

It's that I like my sleep and not his early starts!

# **ATTENTION**

She rubs her bump softly, with strokes and touch

With every compliment made, she gets a small rush.

*'You look radiant', 'You're blooming', 'What a mum you will be!'*

She enjoys the admiring looks, the future they see.

Doors are opened with greetings and a smile

Seats are vacated so she can rest for a while.

She sees the special treatment and preference everywhere she goes

The feeling of admiration and virtue. To those around her, she glows.

She eats without restraint and is never called fat

Strangers begin conversation wherever she's sat.

She's never lonely, even though she's alone

People are cheerful, never down with their tone.

She is young, people take extra care

Buy her refreshment as they see she has little money to spare.

But this girl holds a secret. One hidden from view.

She gets home and takes away her bump that stops her feeling blue.

The cushion is unstrapped, returned to the chair.

It rests neatly for visitors, placed there with care.

Years of invisibility, then her sister a mum-to-be.

She watched as her sibling embraced her new identity.

People loved seeing her, they saw nothing but beauty

She watched in fascination, as strangers saw purity.

Desire for that kindness; she craved that attention.

There must be a means, a route to conception.

No boyfriend to speak of, in fact, she thought she might be gay

So, there was not much opportunity to get in the family way.

She thought the solution was staring at her in the fac

When she was sat on the floor staring into space.

A cushion is plump and easy to mould

It could pass for a belly with the right fold.

She got the parcel tape and began her creation,

There were many attempts at different looks and formation.

The work was complete, the bump looked real.

She found some fitted tops that sealed the deal.

Silliness and experiments aside, would people be fooled?

Or would they sense her deception and become nasty and cruel?

It was a gamble but one she was willing to make

She had nothing to lose, no odds at stake.

So, she went on a bus, headed into town

Catching the looks and compassion from people around.

The girl felt warmth, self-worth, angelic and sweet

She knew courtesy from everyone she would meet.

Life was finally good, she had found a way

To like herself and enjoy each day.

She knew it was false, a devious trick

Moments filled her with dread and a little bit sick.

Would she get caught? Only God knows.

But for now, she would be seen wherever she goes.

# DON'T PANIC WHEN DROWNING

**The Wife**

The time had finally come. With the moment for me to act. So many things have led to this. I must confront him; I will not be a fool anymore. It has slowly been building bit by bit, and I am so angry that he feels any of this is okay. I am his wife. We took vows. Does he not think it has been hard for me too? His body has deteriorated as much as mine, maybe mine is worse after having children. The bikini was RIP as soon as my stomach expanded. And does he not think I have had chances? Okay, maybe not in quite a few years but I have had mild flirtations that may have led to more. I just didn't allow it. I guess that's the difference between us isn't it?

    My suspicions arose when I went to do the washing, and on a white shirt was an unmistakeable smear of foundation. It was the shirt he had worn the day before and I was feeling ill and not wearing makeup that day. Now how does that happen? Ironically, I had been wearing makeup every day for weeks before to try and make him fancy me again. It had been so long since we made love or been affectionate in pretty much any way apart from a quick kiss before trying to sleep. We used to be crazy about one another, neither of us could keep our hands off each other. I felt him slowly slipping away, so I decided to make myself a bit more appealing by trying not to look so goddam tired all the time.

He started to smarten himself up. Putting gel in his hair instead of having it all over the place looking scruffy, he began shaving everyday and moisturising. He started taking early morning runs to improve his body and appear more attractive. He tried more healthy eating and leaving the chocolate bars out of his pack lunch. He was trying to give her the best version of himself.

One night he did not come home until late. There was no accident on the local news, I checked. When he came home, he could not give me any explanation other than 'traffic'.

After that, there was guilt. Flowers for no reason, more attention, something I wanted but instead despised because I knew the true meaning behind it. I have had nothing to do but think about this for weeks. I was onto him from the start. He locks his phone, so I haven't been able to check it, but it has been pinging constantly so she's keen. Well, it will all end tonight, I will confront the bastard and put all my evidence to him. I can't wait to see what he's going to come up with. My hands are shaking uncontrollably, and I feel like my body is on fire, but I must be strong. I deserve so much more.

## The Husband

I don't know what to do. Everything has been leading up to this, and I am scared. I feel like I am making a mistake, what if she doesn't love me and all of this has been for nothing.

I'm unsure if I have been handling this very well. A few months ago, everything felt so intense. I left for the office and it was another day of being ignored. Not even a look or goodbye. My wife doesn't even notice me anymore, I'm a ghost. Lately, she's been wearing makeup. I don't know why but it scares me.

I was quiet all morning and then Debbie, a pretty girl in the office asked me what was wrong. I cried on her shoulder, she kept hugging me. The human contact felt so good, it was so long since I felt any other than a quick peck on the cheek before bed. I love my wife so much. To me, it is as if she has not aged a day and I love being with her. But I feel that she has fallen out of love with me, and I do not know how to cope.

Debbie suggested I make myself a bit more appealing to her, pay her some attention. She asked me, 'Have you tried to make more of an effort?'

I thought about it and I realised I hadn't.

So, I went to Boots the Chemist and bought some hair gel, different deodorant, aftershave and even some moisturiser like David Beckham wears. Anything to break what we were used to. I went next door to the sports shop and bought some running shoes. I used to enjoy running and my wife always used to compliment me on my legs in the early days, so maybe this will help her notice them again.

Whilst I was at the checkout, my phone kept pinging, I tried asking her if she knew how to change settings. My latest phone with all the gadgets sends me notifications about everything from news and weather to updates on my scrabble app. I know it bothers my wife so I thought I would ask if they knew how to turn them off. I may ask the IT guys; any little thing might help.

So, for weeks, I try to improve myself, yet she acts the same. Maybe even colder than usual. I buy her flowers but everything I try is greeted with indifference or anger. Maybe it is too late. Maybe I am fooling myself that she still loves me. I decide on one last big gesture and then one evening I shall come home and surprise her. It is a huge risk, and an expensive mistake but I need to give my marriage everything I got. I made vows after all.

So, I decide to book tickets for us to see her favourite singer, Josh Groban in Barcelona. It would be a couple of days away and give us some time together. Things are always great when we're on holiday. I must stay late at work to secure the tickets and flights, but I hope it's worth it.

I decided to surprise her next week on the anniversary of the day we met, but she sent me a text saying that when I come home tonight, we need to talk. Maybe the surprise will have to be sooner rather than later. I am scared that she'll reject me and tell me we have to part. So many things have led up to this. But the moment for me to act has come. I just hope I'm not too late to save us.

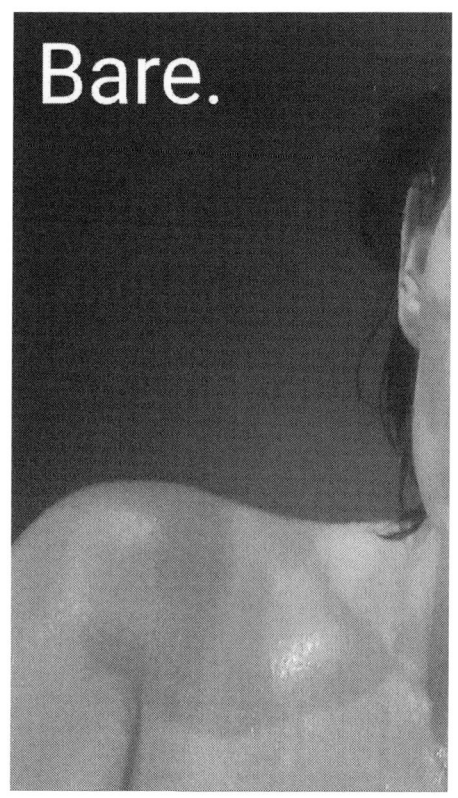

# Bare.

If we laid humankind bare, what would we see?

Cosmetically there is commercialism, greed, lust, gluttony, and a whole lot of things that otherwise might feel like a choice. Humans feed these things outside of them like pets and slowly lose their minds as they watch them grow and, in some ways consume their life and drive. If we allow it, each of these things can become addictive and destructive. Yet everyone has these traits. We only need to do one thing. Control them.

But if you go further and take away the skin, we find we are all the same. We have bones, muscle, blood, veins, no matter where we came from; what we look like on the outside, our choices, or positions in life, we are all essentially the same underneath.

And yet, even though we know this fact, many people feel like an outcast, are tormented, or teased over a distinguishing feature in their outside appearance; something out of their control. They are looked upon and despised with no justification other than a characteristic that makes them unique. Ironically, this same characteristic becomes attractive when becoming loveable to another. The differences that set us apart make us interesting and allow our friends and neighbours to recognise us in a crowd. We pass on those differences to our children so they can adapt them in their own way and make them an evolving combination of our distinction and rarities, along with everyone who came before us.

When our needs are magnified, what are our essential needs?

Water, good diet, exercise, and affection are among the main ones.

Affection comes in many ways, from our parents to the simple acts of friendship. We long for our friends to be kind and to respect and appreciate us. Then we have love. The sensation of a kiss to the touch of a hand. We all crave affection in this way. We need to be thought of as valued, wanted, attractive and that our thoughts and deeds matter to others. The worst thing you can do to affect a person's ego is to constantly ignore them.

A 2012 psychological study carried out at Purdue University found that, without even eye contact from a stranger, people felt excluded and disconnected. A research assistant walked down a populated path and paid no attention to some people and gave others eye contact as they passed them by. The ones the assistant ignored were really affected.

The silent treatment, something many of us do, can have a more serious effect. The anterior cingulate cortex in our brain is responsible for recognising pain. Studies have shown this is activated when people are given the silent treatment. It leads to headaches, digestive problems, fatigue, and insomnia. When the silent treatment is long-lasting, it can lead to more serious problems such as a rise in blood pressure, diabetes and in extreme cases, Cancer.

So, once we acknowledge the need to be 'seen', we must also recognise the necessity of intimacy and sex. Some have these desires more than others but no matter how big or little your sex drive is, we all have certain survival modes.

The urge to procreate and establish our lasting effect on the world is within most of us.

Sleep is another requirement our bodies require to function properly. The only evidence you need of this is to look at a new mother. She is forgetful, overworked, stressed, and tired. She finds it hard to control her concentration which leads to less interaction with others and less able to take care of her other essential needs like eating a wholesome diet or sex.

When we take away the essential parts of us necessary to function, it is then we discover our humanity. Core components of us not vital for our existence but are crucial for maintaining mental wellbeing and happiness.

To become happy, we need to discover what our personal needs are, so we can become the best we can be. For many of us, the satisfaction of knowing we are doing the best we can is all that drives us. Becoming the finest version of ourselves is the goal we all have. For most, our identity is driven by our character, how we treat and help others, being polite and feeling like a valued part of society. We wish to be a person with good morals, kindness, and virtue.

When you strip humanity bare, we find our primary needs are identical, but it is our originality and peculiarities that set us apart.

# **CIRCUS**

The red and white striped tent set the scene and children with their families provided the soundtrack. Smells of roasted nuts, candy floss and popcorn entered my nostrils and made me feel hungry. A gentle reminder of yesteryear and times gone by. I gave my husband the vouchers from the paper, and he stuffed them in his pocket. He momentarily let go of our daughter's hand whilst our teenage son stood the other side of him. My own hand is tugged and jolted as my little boy was jumping up and down.

I recognised and said a quick hello to a couple of friends from the school pick up, both of us knew we were only here for a cheap night of entertainment. They were here in a massive group taking full advantage of the voucher, making memories with families visiting from Somerset.

As I looked around waiting in the queue to enter and take our seats, I glanced behind me. I saw you. It's been 20 years since I last peered into those rich blue eyes. You looked older, but still toned with that body I memorised with touch and smell. I gazed at you and you watched me back. You have a family too. The years were kind to you, and being a dad suits you. We never were old enough for me to wonder if it would.

You have a logo on your t-shirt, but I can't quite see what it is. Should I speak? What should I say? You broke my heart, yet you taught me how to love. I became a woman in your arms.

Suddenly, I am taken back; Nirvana Unplugged on the stereo, Kurt Cobain softly bearing his soul unaware of the tragedy yet to occur and the impact it would have on the world. We lay in bed; you are stroking my arm as the music played and we talked about the future. We smoked cigarettes before they were banned, or we realised just how bad they were.

Our whole lives lay before us, endless possibilities, but the only thing we needed was in that room. Your checked shirt hung on the bedpost as mine lay on the floor. My dolphin tattoo on my left shoulder and your matching fish out of water was the definition of our lives. We would always be different, but we would always be free. Real pain and loss. And yet even with the flash of the last night in my mind, when I looked at you all I felt was warmth. Like an old friend you forgot about and then suddenly see, and it felt like nothing had changed.

I don't still love you the same way, of course, too much time has passed, I have changed and grown. I have become a mother, a wife. I felt thankful that a reoccurring question over many years has been answered. What happened to you? Did you ever wonder what happened to me? The answer was always obvious for both of us of course. We grew up.

It was our turn to buy tickets and I looked away.

Inside we found our seats, and the aisles were busy with children, parents getting snacks and spectators getting comfortable, ready to enjoy the show. We wait, my husband thinks it will all be lame, and the circus won't be overly exciting especially not like he remembers as a kid. He held our little boy on his lap as our daughter quizzed him about different animals and where they lived in the world. Our teenage son sat beside me already bored, as he killed time by playing with his phone.

Out of the corner of my eye, I saw you buying candy floss for your two girls. When you walked away, I watched you move to the other side of the tent and sit with a pretty woman and your son. You looked comfortable, and even though you were sat a little bit away I could still make you out clearly in the bright lights.

You looked around and saw me. We shared a knowing smile, and I could tell you remember me. The lights went down, and the tent darkened. One single spotlight took our attention and life moved on. Just as it always does, and just as it should.

# ALONE

I am alone.

My family is gone.

Now I watch others

Forever forlorn.

My grief is horrendous,

My heart remains unfulfilled.

My body aches for stolen moments,

Our joy eternally stilled.

New chapters and milestones

Feel something amiss.

Life's celebrations dulled,

Undernourished memories of bliss.

Tears come at any time,

Afternoon, evening, or dawn.

Solitude and quiet consume my mind

Yet I smile and carry on.

My family beyond,

My cousins, Uncle and Aunts,

Make me jealous wishing I were their child

So, I could have the closeness that grants.

I have become good at this pretence

My path is waylaid.

Forever alone.

Forever afraid.

## THE MERMAIDS IN THE STARS

There are some people in your life that you always feel a special bond with. In Emily's life, it was her grandmother. She was known to everyone else as Lady, this was because of the way she treated both herself and others. Lady was kind, loving and very respectful of others and most importantly, told the best stories you've ever heard.

    She had silver-streaked hair tied neatly in a bun. She smiled and greeted everyone she knew and even those she didn't. Her wardrobe was an array of long flowing dresses always accompanied by her thick black crocheted shawl. Lady walked along the coast every day with whichever visitor had called in to see her. She gazed in wonder at how beautiful and tranquil the sea appeared. The shimmer and glisten in the water.

    Lady would reminisce about the mermaids she played with on beach holidays when she was young. She missed her school friends, and the mermaidens befriended her; brought her comfort and made her feel safe. How glorious and spellbinding they were. She spoke with sadness about how they all had to journey to the divine ocean above our heads where they could live forever.

One day, she would be reunited with her friends, and they could swim together in the celestial sky. To Lady, the sea was more than a beautiful landscape of endless scope

and wonder, it held a promise. Being close and smelling the saltiness of its essence relaxed Lady and she would gaze at the water. This was her favourite past time. She religiously wore blue ornate jewellery decorated as the sea, so Lady could feel it close around her no matter where she was.

One of the greatest things about Lady was her smell. She always smelt sweet, and when she held your hand, her skin felt silky and soft. You would be grateful for the hugs she gave you and never wanted to let go. Lady's hair felt like white rose petals and her shawl was always gentle to the touch.

Emily found her grandmother as beautiful now as the black and white photos of Lady and her late husband John, in their younger days. Her favourite part of her grandmother were three little lines as big as the width of a middle finger beside her eyes. These to Emily were footsteps of smiles because they only showed when Lady was smiling or laughing. Emily saw them often whenever she was with her.

Although Lady was quite old, she was still mobile after her walks along the coast, so Emily would stay over quite a lot and that is when Lady would tell her stories. One day not long before she died and travelled with the angels, she told Emily something a little different than the usual tales she had grown accustomed to.

'In a little while, not far from now, I'm going to have to go away,' she said. Emily suddenly became frightened.

'Where are you going?' Emily asked in a quivering voice.

'I'm going to go swimming with angelic mermaids in the sky,' she explained. 'It's something I have to do. But I'm looking forward to it. Your grandad is already in the starry sea waiting for me to join him. But don't worry; I will always be with you. Whenever there is a clear black sky, look for the brightest star and there I will be. Talk to me and if you close your eyes and wait for my answer. I will watch and guide you through life, as long as you are willing to listen.'

So that is what Emily did. She was no longer afraid but just kept remembering the stories that her grandmother told her. You see these were no ordinary stories. They made sense of things that Emily didn't understand. Things people always told her that never made any sense. Dotty things grownups would say, silly parent wisdom like an apple a day keeps the doctor away or pick up pennies for good luck. However, soon after visiting Lady's house, they no longer seemed silly, they seemed sort of, well, magical.

She created fables such as the one about a bad-tempered Doctor who scared patients. After digesting apple pips hidden in a pie from an enchantress, he turned into a tree and sprouted leaves from his ears. Or the tale about copper elves who collected tiny metal discs to give to angels who hid inside children's wards in hospitals. The angels would use the shiny copper to reflect light toward heaven, asking fairy Gods to watch over any young patients about to have operations. Whenever Emily heard these 'Old wives' tales' afterwards, they would always make her smile and laugh.

Time passes, Emily is now a grandmother herself and shares the stories with her own grandchildren. They listen and become just as enthralled as she was. Quite often she visited the sea, thought about the mermaidens swimming with her grandparents, and wore Lady's jewellery. Her grandmother guiding her through her hardships and worries, as Emily always listened to the calming sounds and guidance that she felt returned when she spoke silently to the brightest star. Lady became a huge part of generations of the family even though she had passed several years ago. Emily shared her own stories and wore the shawl whenever she missed her. Although it never felt quite as soft, it did always smell sweet.

      Emily walked with her grandchildren along the sea pier, 'when my time has come, watch as the dark blue night twinkles above your head, think of me, and my grandmother. Like Lady, I will always be with you. Never be sad, as I will be happy. Swimming with the angels, the mermaids in the stars.'

## Dear Reader...

First of all, thank you for buying my book. This collection means a lot to me, *Isolation Tales* was my dream, this represents my journey. It has been the biggest challenge I have faced in my writing career so far. Like *Isolation Tales* (my first book), some of the stories or pieces were based on real things, people or places or my own experiences. The rest are of course fictional, but I hope you agree when I state they all have something relevant to say.

If I have made you think, feel emotion, or just forget the world for a while, then I have done my job. Thank you for trusting me to do so.

I have an email address just for readers which you can get in touch with me on. Did a particular piece stay with you and you want to talk about it? Or do you want to let me know you enjoyed/hated the book? You can contact me about anything that takes your fancy, even if it's nothing more than you just want to say hi. Every email goes directly to me, there are no publicists or teams to get through, and I read all my messages. It might take me a little while to get back to you, but I will do my best to do so.

The address is:

MelanieStephens@mail.com


Although this book has been a lot of work, I have learnt so much. And the wonder of an idea forming from a play on words, image, newspaper cutting, or phrase never gets old. I feel so much excitement as I load up my trusty laptop and let the story flow through my fingertips onto the page. That is the joy of being a writer and the magic never dulls. The dream becomes real when someone takes the time to read your work. And that dear reader is your part in my life. You keep the dream alive. Thank you.

*Painting 'Night Dreamer' by Eliza Stephens*

# **Acknowledgements**

To Anita, my angel, my glorious editor. Thank you for every typo corrected, every formatting point, every comment (especially the funny ones), every bit of feedback. You are the master of the written word and I adore you. My star.

To Gavin, there are no words I can use to express how thankful I am to have you by my side. *God only knows what I'd be without you.*

Archie, Eliza, and Hugo, thank you for putting up with me stopping everything to grab a notebook, for spending hours on the lawn, for describing me as an author to your friends and teachers. Being your mum is a privilege I hold dear to my heart.

To Andrea, Pat, Katie, and Charlene, thank you for all your love and support during the whole of my writing journey. I am honoured to call you my closest friends and also my family.

To Mum, Don and Grampie, thank you for inspiring me and shaping me into the woman I am today. I hope I made you proud, and please continue to watch me as I follow my dreams.

To David and Joy Stephens, you both have blown me away by how much love you have shown myself and my work. I couldn't have wished for more. Thank you for being the best hand models I have ever met.

To Gemma Warne, thank you for my cover, you are a creative genius! And for making all the bits and pieces required to make it work. Thank you for getting all my requirements into a single shot! You're an absolute superstar.

To Liz Owen, and everyone at PFLAG National, thank you for all your guidance, help, and source material. Jeanne Manford had an incredible impact on the world, and I hope you feel that I have honoured her courageous story. I am so thankful for the time you have given me, your founder has inspired me so much, and I am grateful I can share moments of her life to inspire others.

The world is thankful for the fantastic work PFLAG does, celebrating diversity, and building a foundation of loving families and support. I hope awareness and tolerance continues to grow and we can soon live in an unprejudiced and non-discriminatory society. Thanks to you, we are so much closer to that goal.

To Kerri Pattinson, thank you for letting me include the poem about Jaime. She was so beautiful and deserves to be celebrated.

To Karen and Johnnie Waugh, Jackie Eastwood, and Natasha McDonald for allowing me to use your images of Notre Dame.

To the residents of my little Cornish village, thank you so much for all your support. You all came out in force, and it is because of you I love where I live!

And finally, to you the reader, my megastars! This book means a great deal to me as do you. Thank you for buying and reading it. I hope you enjoyed it, thank you for being brilliant and awesome.

# About the Author

Melanie Stephens is a full-time writer of fiction. She publishes a variety of short stories and poems regularly on her author Facebook page and posts on her blog Geek Girl Eats Cake.

Melanie lives in Cornwall with her husband and three children. Her first book, *Isolation Tales* was published in May 2020 to raise funds for the NHS Covid-19 appeal. Her story attracted both national and local press and her book received rave reviews.

*The Collection,* is Melanie's highly awaited

second book to showcase her work during

her writing journey so far.

Her next novel is due to come out next year.

You can follow or read more of Melanie's work on:

Facebook @melaniestephenswriter

Blog https://geekgirleatscake.home.blog/

Instagram: @melaniestephensauthor

Scan the QR code below to immediately follow me on Instagram.

If you enjoyed The Collection, why not try…

A Conversation with Melanie Stephens about:

# **ISOLATION TALES**

### Congratulations on the book. Can you tell us a bit more about Isolation Tales?

Thank you, technically it's a novella but that is the reason it is a bit cheaper than most books. This has also allowed me to finish it during the lockdown period.

Isolation tales is a collection of stories and a few poems about the global pandemic, the Coronavirus (Covid-19) and how it has affected the world. There are stories about lots of different viewpoints including keyworkers, parents, children, cleaners, the government, celebrity, even the earth and virus itself. Not just our own country in the UK but all over the world.

### Why write this book at all?

We are living in a historic time. The longest ever living monarch is on the throne, people will look back and talk about this year and what's happened. I thought it was a good idea to produce something that reflects life during this time. Although the stories and characters are fictional, they are based and inspired by interviews with real people, testimonials, reports, and news stories. I wanted to accurately reflect people's experiences. Small details within the stories also reflect little things that have happened during the lockdown, like rainbows in windows and the craze for toilet paper!

### Are the stories hard going then?

Not at all, no. All are easy to read so they accessible to everyone. There's a real mixture as the world is a real mixture of every emotion right now. Some will make you laugh, cry, think and some may show you something that you didn't know before. It's a rollercoaster but hopefully, you will enjoy the ride!

## What was your inspiration for this project as a writer?

I have written a book before, but never to a deadline. I wanted to finish this before lockdown ended. For this reason, traditional publishing was never an option, so I knew I had to use the amazon option instead. I thought I could use lockdown as an opportunity to accomplish something I had never done before; get a book published. That way when I look back at this time, I see it as a good thing and not just as a scary time. If someone needs something, I like to help so I also saw it as an opportunity for me to help the NHS.

## So, this book is for charity?

That's right, every penny that would normally go to the author I am donating to the NHS (National Health Service). Even if you do not like the book, then hopefully people will like they have given to something that we are relying on so heavily right now. I don't think anyone can doubt the dedication and bravery the workers of the NHS have shown during this crisis.

**ISOLATION TALES is available in paperback and eBook from Amazon.**

# MINI COLLECTIVES

During the week leading up to the release of The Collection, I hosted a social media event called The Mini Collectives. It was a vast display of pieces including stories, poems, and photographs that showcased a small selection of the themes and genres within the upcoming book,

Here is a small selection of writing that featured. I hope you enjoy them.

## Woken

I sit in the corner hugging my knees tight to my chest. All is quiet in the darkness, everyone has disappeared, the music has stopped. I have no concept of the time, or how long I have been sat here. Listening for my breaths I do not speak. Stillness. I cannot tell if I am alive or dead. I place my hand upon my chest, and I am relieved when it rises and falls.

I close my eyes, hoping that when the darkness is all I see, it is my own intent and easier to accept. I breathe in and breathe out. Slowly, I must do it slowly. Remembering my exercises, I take a deep breath in and count to five using my fingers.

I whisper, 1, 2, 3, 4, 5.

Hold it.

Breathe out.

Slowly, back from five. I whisper 5,4,3,2,1.

I repeat this process, but this time I talk. My voice fills the room.

'"1,2,3,4,5" hold it.

"5,4,3,2,1."

I do not know if I feel better. I open my eyes. Still darkness. My eyes are not adjusting to the light and remain blind.

I lie down and feel carpet. It's rough, hard, creating a dry embrace that presses against my cheek. My knees rise up to my tummy as I lie on my side. My arms cross my chest. My hair forms a curtain across my face, hiding my fear and solitude.

I do not know what I am wearing but I can feel the carpet on bare legs and arms. The feeling of silk brushes against my skin like a slip.

I start to sing a Green Day song *'Wake me up when September ends'*. My voice sounds haunting within the room as I sing the words, but the music gives me energy and I sing louder.

The song somehow has added meaning and emotion for me than it did before, and I feel like I'm going to cry. I sing with more force and drown the tears with my voice.

Footsteps.

I freeze.

I hold my breath. I hear voices from far away. Male voices. Two of them. The footsteps stop and sounds as if they are fading away. I must not sing anymore as it draws attention.

I roll over onto my hands and knees and force myself to act. I crawl around feeling in the darkness. I tighten my grip on the carpet feeling the rough fibres tense and resist as I pull. I crawl slowly, my knees are already sore, and I want to stop. I force myself to continue. My face feels puffy and my eyes are sore from the tears.

(BANG)

I hit my head on something. Pain shoots across my forehead and I instinctively rub my head hard and fast over where it hit. I raise my hand tentatively upwards and feel wood. An edge square, it's thin. I must have hit a table. A wooden one.

I place my hand over the edge and raise myself up, so I am straight from my knees upwards. I slowly move my hand around on top of the table to see if I can feel anything on it. There is something that slips and moves. A texture different from the wood. I scrunch it beneath my fingers, and realise it is paper. A sheet of paper. I take it. I lean back and place it within my hands. I fold it and place it in my mouth between my teeth. I run my hands down my sides and discover only silk underneath my fingers. As I suspected I have no pockets. I must keep it between my teeth for now.

I lean forward slowly and again hold my hands out and move them around. At first all that welcomes my fingertips is air. I lower my hands and touch the tabletop. I try to see if there is anything else I can feel in the dark.

I touch something. It moves, an echoey clang comes and then my hand is wet. A glass of something. I must have spilt it. I explore searching for the stem and attempt to place it upright on the table. Something pings. I freeze.

    Moving slowly, there is another glass. I glide my fingers lightly around it and follow the solid line. My fingertip runs slowly diagonally down the hard, smooth surface until it hits liquid. I raise my finger to my lips and touch it lightly with my tongue.

I start to shiver as I recognise the taste. And start to scream.

My body tenses as the door opens and light floods the room.

*In the book, love shows itself in many forms. One of the most explored is forbidden love or love that cannot be. I find it fascinating how the main thing everyone wants in life from the moment they are formed, can appear in ways you don't expect or ironically want. One of my favourite poems is Never Seek to Tell thy Love by William Blake. Instead of telling you how great love is, Blake gives almost a warning against following your heart.*

    *The powerful emotion of love, affection, and desire overrides our thought, common sense, and sometimes good judgement. It can take over our minds, bodies, even our lives. It's interesting uncovering new ways love takes control, even when the person you fall for, you know isn't right for you at all!*

## IN ANOTHER TIMELINE

**HIM**

In another timeline, the woman I think so much of

Could have been mine, we could have fallen in love.

In our world we are trapped, we belong to another

We must stick to moments, where we can be lovers.

I cherish each kiss, every promise she makes,

She explains away reasons for the risks we must take.

I quiver under her touch, no matter how small,

If she asked me to be hers, I would leave it all.

We are always on a timer, fleeting moments we seize

We cannot spend a night together or do as we please.

Life can be so cruel when it steals my lady away,

But she knows I am thinking of her every single day.

**HER**

In another timeline, this affair I am part of

Never would have happened, I would have been more in love

with my husband, and not be looking for another

man, to excite me. There would be no need for a lover.

I enjoy our time together, every orgasm he makes

When I become dominant and order him to partake.

He satisfies me. Thankfully, he is not small!

And when we get passionate, he gives it his all!

We do it all over the house, dangerous moments we seize

And down on my knees, I am eager to please!

How long will it last before passion fades away?

For now, we keep going, taking it day by day.

.

*In my stories, I look at ordinary objects and try and see them from their point of view. I enjoy looking at things we take for granted and breathing new life thus creating unique angles to see them.*

## **WHITE BOWL**

Naked in the cupboard

Wearing rings around my side.

A chipped rim, cracked veins, battle scars from long ago.

Waiting in darkness to be brought into the light.

An opening!

Not me. Noise clatters.

The giant hand does not need me yet.


Hot. Burning inside.

Darkness again. Chilled icy air.


Bathed in hot, soapy water.

Roughly scoured, then I stand dripping until dry.

Weight on top of me, keep it centred. Heavy balancing.


My belly is full as dry generous scatterings flow on top of me. Wet drowns and creates mush.

Metal bangs and taps against me then gently tease.

Lifted and carried, but then nothing surrounds me…


I am falling , flying through the…

Shattered.

*A big theme of the book is family and parenting but shown in several different ways and genres. Here is a story about a mum, filling in a memory book for her children. I hope you enjoy it.*

**To my beautiful children,**

**Thank you for giving me this present, it's so lovely you are interested in my life and would like to more about me and hear my memories. The title did throw me a bit at first,** *Grandparents* **book. As you are all under the age of 12, I thought it was a bit soon to throw that title around. As they say, the thought is the main thing, so, I thank you for that (although I do hope the thought was you are interested in mum, and not that you think I look 50 years older than I am! We'll go with the first option, shall we?).**

**My life began,**

**I was born**

**(sorry, you all keep interrupting me and I can't think straight.)**

I was born in a picturesque little village in Devon called Clovelly. It is so precious that people have to pay to visit it. It has a little harbour and is famous for

-You know, I am going a little off track here, but I hope when you are older you all learn the gift of patience. And there are possibilities of waiting for longer than three minutes for a drink or packet of crisps. And just for the record, I know crisps are made from potatoes, but you are not getting your 5 a day from 10 packets of crisps!!! It doesn't work that way, I'm afraid. Wine is made from grapes, but I can't get away with that one either!

So, back to memories.

Yes, Clovelly is really beautiful and was the inspiration for the book *The Water Babies*. I know we don't currently have a copy of the book, maybe I will get one and attach it to this. To be honest, I have never read it. I did see the cartoon and that was quite good. So, you know, something to be proud of.

Lots of things have been filmed there

-Seriously, patience would be a really great thing to have, or the ability to notice when someone is doing something. As a result, you may realise maybe right this second isn't the time to ask if worms have eyes or ask me how many bridges there are on planet Earth!

As Clovelly is so pretty, my Aunty still lives there. We don't see her much. To be honest, she's a bit annoying, but you may meet her one day. I enjoyed my first few years at Clovelly. I lived there till I was about ten. Then we moved to another place in Devon, called Exeter.

We have been to Exeter lots of times. Your grandparents still live there now. As you can imagine, it was quite a change

(I don't know what technology is like in your time, but I am hoping you do not get screens freezing like crazy like now, or you come up with a better solution than simply turning it off and on again. I have to do this umpteen times a day, it is very irritating and frustrating. You guys need me to do it so much. I have shown you how, but apparently, none of you can press a button and hold it down. Yet you have no problem at all building a rabbit fortress in Minecraft!

I am guessing none of you will work with machinery as a career. If so, God help us all.)

Anyway, we moved to this big place

-I know I keep banging on about it, but patience children! The ability to wait without pulling a face or complaining and tormenting others is a really big bloody virtue and so for the record, is not annoying your mother.

I hope when it is your turn to look after me, I am old and helpless, and you have to do a milelong list of chores that cannot wait. Or, when you have children and become parents yourselves they are little shits that eat nothing but chicken nuggets and pizza and inform your dentist that you do not make sure they brush their teeth twice a day every day. Thus, leaving you to explain that to get ready for school you take twenty minutes to put a bloody sock on, so you always run out of time.

Anyway, I digress. Exeter is massive and it was a big change. I didn't enjoy school. My sister Faye was however brilliant at everything and was in all the school sports teams, as well as a hoard of after school clubs. She ran cross-country for the county, and hockey for Exeter. I was only okay at the 100m run at sports day, and even then, I would arrive somewhere in the middle. I really hope the genes do a side skip cause your dad was useless at sports too. I was more interested in smoking in the toilets and drinking 20/20 down the park with my mates. So, I guess you could say I was an irresponsible child.

Your dad was a complete geek without the smarts, he just mucked about too. Faye now runs a successful recruiting business and earns lots of money. So, stay away from 20/20 and cigarettes. And drugs. And cabbage.

(That day you all tried it and we all had to endure a less than fresh room that even the smelliest candle couldn't fix was a nightmare. Four of those Winter Spice beauties burnt for hours trying to disguise the smell. Your bottoms were rumbling all afternoon and evening, it was one of the worst Christmas Day's in our family history. It didn't help you all kept blaming Grandma for it. Every time you asked her if she loved to toot, I had to cover for you all by asking if she would like a marzipan fruit instead! We got through four boxes that year. The combination of cabbage and sprouts was a dangerous concoction that shall never be repeated!)

Somehow both myself and your father scraped into Exeter University, which is where we met and fell in love. Your dad thought he was going to have an easy time of it if he studied Photography. Most of his pictures were a last-minute panic after one too many late-night sessions of Dungeons and Dragons with boys from down the hall. Later on, he didn't do the assignments because he went on dates or time spent with me.

I studied Mechanics, as I wanted to save money on my car when it needed fixing. I thought cars would always be around, so it was a good career. Since then, unfortunately, I have forgotten everything (including according to your father how to parallel park). But I can always re-train if the time is right.

Now I have to change the chargers for your tablets as they are all at 4% but I hope you all found this interesting. I will fill in the rest of the book sometime soon. I hope you are all good people. Kind and thoughtful to others. I do love you all. You're my greatest accomplishment if I am honest. When you grow up, don't move away too far. I would miss you. And give me an impromptu hug once in a while, okay? I'd like that.

Love you all,

Mum x

*One of the ways I gained inspiration was by drawing on past personal experiences that shaped who I am today. A big life moment for me came when I conquered my ultimate fear. I remember vividly how scared I was yet also what was at stake if I did not achieve my goal. The Collection is very much a journey of work that defines me and key moments. Hidden within the stories is a seed of truth about myself or something I am passionate about. A big part of being a writer is laying yourself bare and sharing your world with others. To commemorate this, I would like to share this story.*

## **OVERCOMING FEAR**

When it came to the anniversary of my Grandad's death, I wanted to do something special. He was extremely important to me. He was a simple man, yet his honest kind nature made him an incredible one. We believed in each other and held one another on a pedestal so high compared to others. He died from cancer and spent his last days in a hospice. I saw the difference these places made to the families going through the worst points in their lives and so helping them seemed a good idea as a way to honour him.

I wanted to raise lots of money to help, but I knew the only way to do that was to attempt something big. I tried to think of the worst thing I can imagine. I came up with two: holding a tarantula as I hate spiders or jumping out of a plane.

I am petrified of heights, absolutely terrified of them. But if I wanted everyone to give, I needed to do the biggest challenge I could think of and for me, this was the plane. It was remarkably easy to organise, I just had to see if I could do the date I wanted. My husband got quite the shock when he came home, and I announced I am going to jump out of a plane on August 31st. However, after the shock and accusations of craziness passed, he understood why I needed to do this.

My mum got involved and tried to get as many sponsors as she could. I did the same, and the theory worked. As so many people knew my fear they gave generously. The Hospice and their team gave me instructions and a t-shirt to wear along with photos to take.

On the day I was lucky. I had bright sunshine after rain all week. Both my youngest children had the day off school and my mum travelled down to be there. I designed a t-shirt featuring my Grandad's photo to wear so it was no mistake who all this was for. I took part in the safety meeting and met my tandem flier, Andy.

As we got into the plane, I was shocked to see the door missing. Immediately I questioned it, and I was told it was for safety! They laughed when the saw my face and promptly sat me closest to it. As soon as the plane took off, I couldn't look out of the hole in place of the door. It was noisy and cramped, and I was sitting in a very comprising position on a stranger's lap. Everyone was warned there would be a time when you could no longer back out, it was five minutes before when you needed to get into position to roll out.

Up to this point, I was laughing and joking with the guys on the plane and then as we passed the point of no return, it was only then it dawned on me what was happening. Fear consumed every part of me as I realised, I could die, and for the first time, I didn't know if I could do it. And then another realisation entered my head.

The thought was exactly what would have been at the forefront of my Grandad's mind if he knew what I was about to do. It was of the families this money was going to. The help and care they would receive in the timeless hours that they hated but dreaded ending. The pain and heartache, the loss. I was taken back to the last day my Grandad spent in this world. I was with him; I was the last word he spoke. The kindness the carers had shown, the way they took care of me as I could not take care of myself. Every thought was consumed with how petrified I was to lose the man I loved so deeply, yet not wanting him to suffer a moment of pain.

In the plane, I felt all the emotion of those final hours. The money could pay for more carers, supplies, family comforts and so much more. I saw children, mothers, fathers, grandparents, and knew I couldn't take away my chance to help them.

A voice told me to get out of the plane.

And I did.

To me, it was scarier letting all those loved ones down. If I could make one moment of pain easier then I had to try and do so.

To this day, getting through that moment is the bravest thing I have ever done. I screamed until I knew I wouldn't die and hated every second of the jump, but I am also proud.

I did justice to my Grandad by helping others and that was worth every second of fear.

*I like to challenge perspectives of people we think we know. It's enjoyable to see how far I can go with the characters and place them in difficult situations. Maybe even entice the reader to continue their story in their head, giving them the power to decide my character's fate. Here is a good example.*

Dear God,

O' Heavenly Father, I need you to hear my prayer. I am a good catholic, I have tried to spread the good word and live by your teachings. But now I need your guidance Lord and your forgiveness.

     I have unkind thoughts and I fear I must go against everything I stand for. I have been firm, rallied in your name, Lord, about the sanctity of life. I have stood outside in the rain, cold, frozen until my hands shook, trying to persuade expectant mothers and whores to not murder their child. I proved these clinics and hospitals are performing mass destruction against the voiceless and innocents. I have shown the world we need to give babies the chance of life so rightfully theirs. But now dear lord I need your strength as I am afraid that I must become one of these women. I have no choice Heavenly Father. Please forgive me. I am with child and I cannot keep it. I know children are a heritage from the Lord and I thank you for my reward. But I do not know if I can accept it.

The gift you have bestowed is not my husbands. He is not warm or loving. He calls me cold-hearted and cruel, which hurts me, Lord. I know you see how it pains me when he says such things. He tells me we are married and therefore cannot part, but that does not mean he must like living with me. Yet Joseph is kind and says I smile warmly. He tells me that I bring him joy. I know you approve of Joseph. We began our affection at Catholic School after we learnt of Jacob, and his cousins Leah and Rachel. And also, Esau and his cousin Mahalah. The union between us has been sacred, a secret between ourselves, Father Andrew, and the Holy Trinity.

My husband knows nothing of the relationship between myself and my cousin. If I have the child you have graciously given us Lord, he will know. I believe he will not leave as divorce is forbidden, but he will tell our families. My parents, and his, my Aunt and Uncle. I have to think about Joseph's family including his children. People can be cruel, dear Lord, and may not understand our union.

I need your help, O' Heavenly Father. Please guide me and show me the way forward. Must I commit the ultimate sin and murder my child? Help, me as I cannot see another way. If I have to do this, can be baptised once more to cleanse me of my sins? Please show me a sign, how must I act? I am at your mercy. Heavenly Father, please hear my prayer.

In the name of the Father, the Son, and the Holy Spirit. Amen.

## THREE STORIES OF CHRISTMAS

*One thing I do like to do which is featured in the upcoming book, The Collection, is looking at different experiences, yet they have the same thing at their core. Considering the time of year, I decided to write three mini-stories about Christmas. All of these are inspired by real events.*

1. A Pause in War
   Carols travelled over the earth, men exchanged tobacco, hats, and food. One man knelt in front of another as he cut his hair. A soldier snipped away at the threads of another man's buttons and did the same with his own. They placed them in each other's hands with a message of thanks. Gatherings of men from different lands spoke of stories of home, and what they left behind. Sweethearts, motorbikes, homecooked meals and good homes.
   
   A week before, these men were enemies. Soon they would be enemies again, but in 1914 for a short period, they lay down their weapons and came together to celebrate Christmas. They brought peace and a welcome break of the horror that had been endured for months before. They wrote letters home to loved ones confessing they wouldn't miss this unique and weird Christmas for anything. For that fleeting period, the guns were silenced, and instead impromptu games of football were played.

2. Christmas in the USA
   Chris took a walk through his little quaint hometown. He ventured down Comet Street, Cupid Avenue and came into Bethlehem. You may think we are within Chris's imagination or playing with toys in a map he made at school but in fact, Chris lives in Florida, America. Chris's hometown is Christmas. Every day on his daily walk, Chris passes a massive 200ft crocodile outside a jungle adventures theme park. A huge contrast to the year-long Christmas tree standing proud beautifully decorated. Or the permanent nativity scene or festive gift shop. Now, word has got out, Christmas has become a favourite tourist destination for many, it boasts the largest cypress forest in the state and Chris writes letters to Santa all year round.

3. The gift of £50

The shoppers browsed and did their shopping. Many had already gone into the supermarket once that week, but supplies ran low, special dinners needed to be made and children had run out of things for their pack lunches.

There was one shopper who was not there to shop, instead, he was there to find people. One by one he chose the people who stood out to him for small reasons. They had a nice smile, they looked poor and on hard times, or he was just drawn to them.

One by one he approached without them being aware, they carried on shopping. He slipped the envelope into their trolleys and hurried away before he could be seen. Eventually, each of the chosen arrived at the till and discovered what he had done.

Inside each envelope was a £50 note and a letter:

> 'I recently came into a windfall. It is more than my family and I need so I wanted to spread the wealth and make your Christmas a little easier. This is not a trick, there's no hidden cameras or catch. Just have a Merry Christmas.'

Every recipient's day was brightened, and they never forgot the stranger's kindness. Some re-examined how they helped others and swore to do better, others just had a great story to tell that made them smile and feel warm every time they shared it.

*My favourite story at Christmas is without doubt, A Christmas Carol by Charles Dickens. I feel it brings such joy to the heart and really shows what the season is about. Being kind and enjoying the love of your fellow man. When I found out about the story of Dr Miles Marley, Charles Dickens, and a connection with Cornwall, I couldn't resist creating a little story. Merry Christmas!*

## Grigor and Marley

Grigor was the oldest elf. He had been around for centuries, and like so many other elves he will continue to live forever as God intended his world to be full of magic and all things good. The smartest decision he had made was Santa Claus. He had conquered his role better than Grigor had ever imagined. People adored him and he really gave the elves a good image that was so easy to love. Before Santa, Christmas was a lot lower key. Grigor handed out fruit and coal to homes around the world. But at that time, it was still a wondrous and incredible gift to receive.

Grigor poured the hot milk which was now bubbling on the stove and added nutmeg and, cloves to the mixture and stirred. A cinnamon stick bounced around the creamy liquid and seemed to welcome the new additions. Grigor bent down and took a deep breath in. The smell was glorious, and he was excited to have it but made himself be patient.

He went to the cupboard and took out a grey pewter tankard and placed it beside the pan. Then he came into the next room with his chair and book of A Christmas Carol placed gently on the chair. The fire crackled beside him. He glanced at his watch and came back to the stove. The drink was ready. Grigor poured the mixture into his tankard and came and sat down. He placed his drink on a little side table beside him and picked up his book. He had read it over and over but never grew tired of the story.

As he began the tale, he opened the page to reveal Marley's Ghost and his mind travelled. He remembered the day Marley came into Charles Dickens's head. It was long ago and thanks to a Physician based in London, who then lived in a little English County called Cornwall….

It was St Patricks Day in Westminster, and Dr Miles Marley was having a party to celebrate. The guests arrived in their finest gowns and attire looking forward to an interesting evening. One of the most anticipated guests was the popular and always animated author Charles Dickens.

Marley and Dickens heard of each other through mutual friends and were yet to meet. The author arrived promptly and mixed with the guests. Apart from a quick greeting at the door, Dr Marley could not speak to his special guest until dinner when they were all sat down.

They began with a creamed potato and cauliflower soup, and conversation flowed freely. After the soup bowls had been cleared away and the wine glasses topped up, Dr Miles Marley spoke about the chatter of his guests toward the author.

'Mr Dickens,' he began in a raised voice. 'I do enjoy your books, but I was wondering where you came up with your ideas? How the Devil do you know what to write about?'

Mr Dickens chuckled. 'Why, the world around us provides much inspiration. You only need your eyes open and be aware of the surroundings in order to benefit from it. People walk around blind. I always find it strange for instance, how little notice, good, bad, or indifferent, a man may live and die in London...'

'I think I am happy not to notice the bad men,' interrupted a young lady sat opposite Mr Dickens. 'Otherwise, I shall find London a lot more terrifying place to live. I shall have to move to the country and paint trees!'

The Lady's remarks were greeted with chuckling among the guests.

'My dear lady,' replied Mr Dickens smiling. 'If there were no bad people, there would be no good lawyers!'

The guests laughed.

'May I ask Mr Dickens, what are you working on now?' the young Lady asked.

The table all chorused her request, and Charles Dickens smiled.

'I do have a little tale brewing,' he began. 'But it is still at the early stages. I am still forming the story. The characters are appearing to me as we speak.'

'Now?' asked Dr Marley. 'Is that how it works?'

'Indeed. The hard part is finding their names,' smiled Mr Dickens.

'How do you normally acquire them?' inquired Dr Marley.

'I get inspired, Dr Marley. By people.'

'So, you would just use the people you meet?'

'Yes, Doctor Marley,' explained Mr Dickens. 'It has proved most effective in the past.'

'Have you used any of us here tonight?' the young Lady enquired with a smile. 'Mind you, I think our host is safe!'

The room chuckled. Dr Marley most of all. 'Yes, Felicity. I do believe Marley would be most unsuitable for a Dickens book. Pickwick has a rhythm to it, don't you agree? And Marley is not nearly as interesting as Barnaby Rudge or as dastardly as Fagin. No, I believe I shall never have the good fortune.'

'On the contrary Dr Marley, I believe Marley is an excellent name and from the moment I received your kind invitation to dine tonight I thought with your permission, of course, I would use it. It would be perfect for my new story.' Mr Dickens took a sip of wine and savoured his moment. 'In fact, by the end of the year, Marley will be a household name!'

And Charles Dickens was right. A Christmas Carol turned out to be the most successful book of the 1843 holiday season. Soon after the St Patricks Day Dinner, Dr Miles Marley moved to Cornwall where he entertained Mr Dickens many a time. Mr Dickens was a fan of the county and featured it in several scenes of A Christmas Carol. Dr Marley enjoyed the story of Scrooge for ten Christmases to follow but passed away in his home at Port Isaac shortly after.

Grigor sipped his spiced milk and read into the night. He, like Dr Marley, never thought his name was special. But Grigor found and mentored the man who brought the magic into Christmas. There are always the big stars of tales, such as Santa and Ebenezer Scrooge. Both of these men are considered the spirit of Christmas to so many. But behind them, at their beginnings are the people who set them on their way, like himself and Jacob Marley. No matter how ordinary you believe yourself to be, you can help others achieve greatness, guide them on their way. You never know the impact you can bestow. Especially at Christmas.

## **DEFINED AND INSPIRED**

*Remembering past defining moments while being inspired to create enchanting and engaging new ones for your reader.*

*This defines my world and journey as a writer.*

Printed in Great Britain
by Amazon